LIVING AND LOVING JESUS

A Life Lived Being Christian

Pastor Steve Orsillo

Dedication

I DEDICATE this book first to my wife Vicki who lived it with me and inspired me with her faith and absolute commitment to follow Jesus. She is my best friend and partner through this life of being Christian.

Secondly, to my children Nicole, Mark, Danielle and Anthony, my babies. The Lord gave you to me, to cause me to be a better man. You have inspired me by your hearts and your love. I am so proud of each of you!

Contents

CHAPTER 1

Living and Loving Jesus

MY PASTOR, Joe Wittwer would commonly say, "Just keep loving Jesus and He will take care of the rest." Well 'the rest' has turned out to be quite a story, and I must say that I was so very fortunate to have had a pastor who would teach me such a lifelong truth. My favorite question to ask some people is, "are you living and loving Jesus?"

In 1986, I had a particularly tough time in the ministry and decided to get my contractor's license. I had been in construction since I was 18 years old and I had been doing ministry since 19. In 1986, I was 30 years old and had my third child. I had been a foreman on most jobs and worked it around my ministry for many years, then since it became evident that having my own company was going to be better pay and more flexible time constraints, I started Steve Orsillo Construction and as Forest Gump said, "God showed up." We were blessed, for the first time we had money in the bank.

The ministry on the other hand was painful and I was surely suffering. So I sat out, it would only be for a season but I said, "if the Lord calls me I will come."

He had lost my number or so I had thought, so I focused my love for God on giving and my business on leading trades-people to Jesus, business was good.

One day He did call, we were moving and we did not know where. In my business I had invested in a house in Oroville. The Gulf war began and this house would not sell, it was on a incredible 5 acres with a view of the ends of the earth, you could almost see heaven from there.

We discussed Oroville as the city of our destiny but I had said these words to my wife, "the last place that I want to move is Oroville, I have played baseball up there all my life and it is a horrible town!" I proceeded to drive to Oroville to check on that house, which is about an hour and a half drive. When I came to the driveway to the house the Lord spoke to me. He said, "this is where I have you and this is what I have for you, Oroville." I said first, "yes Lord this is all that I have ever wanted, just to know Your will." Then I said, "You're going to have to tell Vicki because I just told her how bad Oroville is." So I called her and asked, "did the Lord speak to you since I left?" She answered, "He said were moving to Oroville." She rented the U-haul truck as I drove home, and we proceeded to load up and move to Oroville, California. We arrived in Oroville at 1am. The next morning I unloaded and was living in Oroville, mid September of 1991. The next thing that I said to the Lord was, "okay, we are here, now what are we here for?"

CHAPTER 2

Renewal

THE MINISTRY of giving and leading people to Jesus continued to be blessed and the vocation of avoiding the professional ministry was also blessed. Yet, what had become a small hole in me or a missing link in the value structure of Steve Orsillo, this giving your life away part of the cost of abundant life, that bank account was being over drawn, and the abundant life was becoming a burden or an ache in my soul. I was wounded and didn't know it nor had I even considered it. What I did believe was that I was thirsty. The living water was not flowing in my life, soon giving had no joy. Not being able to increase my giving was causing me to become a religious giver, not a freely it has been given so freely give from the abundance kind of giver.

Teaching people in the market place to experience God in a short prayer stopped having any joy. It's what we do, it felt like a job, it did not feel like ministry. Sure, I was leading worship and using my skills for the benefit of my pastor and church. Soon I was becoming hard hearted and less like who I used to be. Was I counting the cost properly, was the cost in money hurting the part of me that was beautiful and causing me to become hard and religious? I do know this, I was dry. Giving money, which can be the greatest thing had become a prideful thing, even distasteful.

Then I had an experience. I was sitting at a stoplight in the pouring rain and saw the place where a man who had injured me and robbed me as a teenager had worked and I started to imagine if I saw him, what I would do. Well, I began to beat him in my mind and proceeded to kill him in my imagination. When I came out of my dream, my truck all fogged up, I did not know how many green lights I had missed. I finally knew that I was broken and needed to be fixed. So I prayed, I cried out to Jesus, "I need help."

Soon after this I went to a Foursquare summer camp. I had volunteered to take the kids up there from our church and stay to help because I had been a youth pastor at that camp for many years and was well known.

As I drove there my continual prayer was, where is your living water? Lord where is it, I am thirsty? Then one day at the camp I saw a group of pastors at a picnic table and went over to them. One of them was telling about some experiences that he had when he went to a church in Toronto, Canada. I listened casually until he said that this church had been called a "watering hole to the world". My heart leapt inside me and I called my wife and asked her to buy me a ticket to Toronto.

Is it possible to find this living water once you have gotten away from it? I prayed, "Lord I am living in a dry and parched land and I don't know how to find YOU, the Living Water."

I went to this church in Toronto. It is the Toronto Airport Christian Fellowship. On the first night the speaker stopped his message and said, "the Lord wants to say this to someone, hear His word," and he continued, "you are living in a dry and parched land and if you will come to me I will renew you and fill you, and living water will begin to flow from you again and the latter days will be for you greater than the former days. I have called you to be a fountain of blessing to others."

Well, I ran to the front and so did many others who were also dry and thirsty. Like a man who is dying of thirst, crawling in the desert I drank deep of the river of my God and I WAS BORN AGAIN, AGAIN right there on that carpet, I was renewed.

The short story is that after that day, I fasted a lot, I prayer walked a lot. We spent our energy, we spent our time, we didn't eat, we walked and sought God. We pleaded with the Lord, "come to our city, show us how to receive, heal our faith." The cost to our lives was not something that we could measure or even see at the time, the net result was that we received abundant life.

"*Give and you will receive.*" It works with life, it works with time, it works with energy, it also works with the fruit of the spirit as Jesus said, "blessed are the merciful for they shall obtain mercy." GIVE, this is Jesus' example. GIVE, it may cost you everything, look at Jesus, He did die, He was not rescued from the suffering. The apostle Paul said that he had not suffered like Jesus suffered yet, so how could he complain. It may cost for a season but "*joy comes in the morning.*" I was not looking to return to the ministry, I had no secret wish to pastor a church, but God called. He had my number, I said, "yes Lord."

I thought that it was going to be a church of renewal to the middle class of Oroville. In a store front, very visible to the community. But GOD! He had a plan for me that was so much more abundantly rewarding. It was a journey that if a man knew the cost of before setting out, he might just procrastinate the first step until the season passed him by. This plan had plenty of joy and reward as well as suffering and even a few dark nights of the soul.

CHAPTER 3

The Father's House

THE CALL of God to start a church in the poor section of our city was, to say the least, a shock. I had not even driven through this section of town except for in the most dire necessity. To my wife and me the call of God is all we needed. To know His will is to know our future.

Our work began with the plan to build a pastel colored Vineyard Church with the blessing of the Church Planting Coach in our area. The Lord changed our whole plan and sent us to a bible study at an old fire house which was in the south side of Oroville. There were fourteen people at this bible study and they asked me, "would you be our pastor?" My wife Vicki and I asked each other what the Lord was saying about all of this and we agreed, this was God's plan and this bible study was going to be The Father's House Church. It also became obvious to us that we were not going to be a Vineyard Church. Instead, it would be revealed what our affiliation was going to be. It wasn't long before it became clear that we would join Partners in Harvest.

Partners In Harvest is an association of churches and leaders. It brings us together with pastors and leaders that have also been touched by the Father's love and the blessings of the Holy Spirit which was poured out in Toronto, Canada on January 20th, 1994. We share core values and similar experiences with each other and most of us would say that our ministries have been the best and most fulfilling since the first time we got touched by the love of God in Toronto.

I recently went to a Partners gathering at Toronto Airport Christian Fellowship in Toronto where several hundred of us gathered for a pastors and leaders conference. Several friends asked me what I thought was different about this pastors conference from others that we have attended.

I told them about the family. I had been to many pastors conferences and never had a feeling of family been so evident. They care about your struggles and they genuinely wish you well. This crowd is not jealous or in competition with each other. They care about you and your ministry. When one hurts they come to the rescue. They reach out to each other in a real way. Their generosity to each other is beyond anything that I have seen anywhere else. They testify about their ministry as an honor to God and they love Jesus and worship Him unashamedly. The most incredible thing about the Partners in Harvest gathering is the stature of the people that you are serving with. Every time I talked with someone I was amazed to find out who they were.

A small sample of this is that in two days I met people whose ministries include orphanages in Kenya, training Nigerian pastors in Norway to send back to Africa and a mission in the Sudan by a guy who sold all that he had and moved to the Sudan. In the last three years he has had forty-five thousand people come to know Jesus and has them in churches that he has planted in their villages. His church in Washington that supports him is no bigger that forty-five people. That's a forty-five to forty-five thousand return.

I met a seventy plus year old couple that travel to very difficult to reach places like India and Zambia to minister the Father's love to leaders.

There are missions in Ghana. In Nicaragua one pastor runs a mission that feeds the elderly of a city, all while he pastors his church in Minnesota. A pastor in Tulsa is planting churches in Chile.

One couple got up to share about going to churches in the Islamic world where the ushers have to carry weapons and any man carrying a bible will disappear from the earth.

There were two men who drive six days in a Land Rover and then go on camel from there to minister in North Africa to people that Christians are not allowed to visit.

There is Fred Wright and Dan Slade who travel the world visiting and supporting the churches, and organizing these conferences. They try to help each pastor feel special, which is a gift in itself. Story after story of people giving their lives for the gospel, the greatest group of people that I have ever met!

John Arnott is there, who has given us leadership in this revival, as well as the most important message of our time, *The Importance of Forgiveness*.

It is common at these pastor conferences to have Roland Baker, a man who with his wife Heidi has changed the spiritual face of Africa with some say a million salvations and countless miracles, planting six thousand churches.

I have wished all my life to know people with this kind of faith and personal testimony. Yet here in Partners in Harvest the room is full of these giants of the faith. I have only been able to tell part of it, and only some of them can come to conferences. There are so many more stories that it would take whole books to describe. I'm sure that these books will be written and the Partners in Harvest legacy will be talked about for many generations to come.

CHAPTER 4

A Ministry to the Poor

THE MINISTRY to the poor in the Western world may not be the same as it is in the rest of the world. In the United States I have found that the people that we would call poor do not compare with those who live in South America or Mexico. In the U.S. poverty seems to cause a taker-mentality or entitlement attitude, not to mention that the standard of living that we call poor compared to the standard of living of the poor in Africa and other impoverished nations does not even look the same. In the U.S. because of the incredible financial blessing we have enjoyed for many decades, the poor have suffered from the same conditions as the rich have.

The principalities over nations don't discriminate between the poor and the rich, the haves, and the have-nots. They inflict hopelessness and emptiness across the board equally. They offer different medicine to ease the pain in whatever form you want it. All of them are rooted in the same garden: selfishness.

Selfishness is to me the number one fruit of ungodliness. The number one fruit of godliness is love. When you read 1 Corinthians 13 you can clearly see that it is best defined in English as selflessness. If selflessness is to be the number one evidence that Jesus is the Lord of someone's life and its fruit is that which we are to examine, then selfishness would be the number one fruit of a godless society. If we examine the poor neighborhoods of our cities and look at the people we would call poor, we will see that a pattern of selfish behavior is the rule in the dysfunctional people amongst them. In the pursuit of self-gratification they ignore the needs of their neighbors, their friends, and their families until they find themselves in a state of misery and decay that they are helpless to change.

My experience is that selfishness is the root of all of society's sickness, including hate and all fleshly pursuits. The issues of the heart like betrayal, abandonment and abuse foster excesses of all kinds, like drug and alcohol addiction, which continue the cycle of selfishness. In fact, if you look into someone's affliction and pain, you will most often hear a testimony of a selfish lifestyle, theirs and the people around them on a level that most people would be horrified by.

The manifestation of selfishness shows up in so many diverse ways, such as the abuse mentally, physically, emotionally and sexually, of people who are weaker than the abuser. This gives the abuser power or pleasure or even a possession that they have coveted.

Selfishness is also the number one cause for the abandonment of children. There is great soul pain in this life of self-service. This leads to the use of substances that numb the pain, deep pain that was passed down to them from the selfish abuser that taught them this way of life. In all situations of dysfunction where people are miserable you will find a root of selfishness. It is the mother of shame, pride and the perpetrator of all fleshly desires that bring devastating destruction to God's wonderfully created children.

Another example that selfishness is the root of all dysfunction is the society that ignores the people who suffer from poverty and blames them for their situation. They would rather do nothing or let someone else do something, this way the more fortunate don't have to give anything of themselves to the people we would call poor. This builds resentment and division for everyone and in the process everyone loses. A cycle of mistrust and then hate begins to grow and we become completely divided.

In a ministry to the poor I believe with all my heart that this understanding is the key to the kingdom of God. The poor as I have defined them are reached, not by trying to be like them physically or relating to them by talking their language. They are reached by talking God's language. They receive, when love as defined in God the Father and the Lord Jesus is shown to them. *"For God so loved the world that He gave His son." "For the joy set before Him He endured the cross."* This is the love of God and it is spelled: selflessness. If the dysfunctional poor are defined as selfish, and God's love is defined as selflessness, then what people need is God's love.

Since most of them come looking for what Christianity can give them instead of coming to bring their life as a gift to Him, we must show them a life that is given over to the Lord, a life that is given away for the blessing of others. If we who minister to the poor won't give our lives away as Jesus did then who will ever break this cycle of selfishness that has the western world completely bound up.

We must teach them to give their life away based on the principles that Jesus taught about. *"Give and you will receive."* This works with money; if you want more money then give what you have away. This doesn't make any sense at all if it's not a Godly pursuit, but insert the miraculous power into a life given to God, and then it makes perfect sense. If it works with money then would it work with time?

My wife and I run a construction company. We have a property management company that manages 40 properties and we pastor a church of 350 people. We also have four children. People often ask us how we do it? Yet, our answer would actually be that it's easy. In fact we probably spend more time alone together than most couples, we have more spare time than I can even believe.

Our children say that it's hard to believe but their parents have been there for them. These children are the best people that I know, gifted beyond even my imagination. We truly are blessed in an abundant way and we give away more of our time than we could possibly afford. If this principle of giving works with money and time then how does it work with life?

Our daughter Danielle, who is our third child, grew up with her older brother being almost four years older than her yet he was only one year ahead of her in school because her brother Mark has Down's Syndrome and is developmentally delayed. She developed a closeness to him that was very special.

When she went away to Arizona State University on a basketball scholarship, she began working with developmentally disabled adults. It was very moving to see groups of her clients at her college basketball games cheering her on and after the game she would run up into the stands to greet them. The sports magazine Sports Illustrated was highlighting student athletes for their character and their work in their communities and they published a piece on our daughter Danielle, complete with a picture of her and her friends from the Day Program.

I am proud of all my kids when they are great at something and she is a fantastic basketball player, yet I am much more proud of the fact that Danielle was honored for her love of people who have disabilities and the fact that she genuinely gives love to people and really doesn't do it for a benefit but truly gives her life away. Life comes to those who give life and not just any life but they receive life abundantly.

Looking around me I see a lot of people that don't seem to be having an abundant life, and they wonder why they don't experience all of the promises that should be there from their belief in Jesus.

What I would ask them is where are they giving their life away? If you want abundant life then give your life away or lay it down for your brother, *"give and you will receive, pressed down shaken together and running over, good measure will you receive."*

You can apply this principle to every aspect of life and if we teach this to our people they will begin to see an abundant return of their time, money and life, they will begin to see selflessness or Godliness as a most evident fruit in their life. It is the evidence of their Christianity. This process takes a lot of time and effort but as it begins to take hold, the fruit is unbelievable. The best part is the multiplication, as this fruit becomes wonderful sons and daughters who start focusing their attention on their loved ones and neighbors with a desire to give them what they have received.

The harvest becomes plentiful. The reward is being surrounded by life, it compounds and duplicates more like a snowball effect than anything else that I can describe. It happens if we come at the problem in the opposite spirit, selflessness at selfishness. Give our life for them, ask them to give their life for others, then the others give their life and a new cycle is born. One that brings life, which builds on life and so on.

The next most important issue in the ministry to the poor is the lack of fathers and mothers. There has been such a lack of effort in the homes to try and guide or lead people as children, resulting in them becoming adults who have no ability to be directed in any way. The average person in need of our ministry has a pattern of rebellion that starts showing up in very early childhood and before long every authority figure has punished them in some way. Teachers, principals and soon law enforcement and judicial authorities have added their attempts to correct the wrong direction that these ones are going. Then add the misuse of that authority by some and now they have justified their distrust of all authority. The only person that they will trust is themselves, with absolutely no reason, since the worst leader that they have ever had is themselves.

A young man named Devin came to our church to join our youth group. He was the most misfit young man that I had ever met. He had purple hair cut to look as silly as possible and whenever his hair stopped getting attention he would change the color or wear pink furry slippers. In whatever event or program we would try to run he would disrupt until we would have to stop. Hardly ever did we have a function with any success as long as Devin was there. I had on several occasions, when it was clear that a person was not with us to receive but to rob others, determined that they were robbing others and told them not to return and we would leave their seat empty.

This is where I was with Devin. I asked to talk with him, to explain that he just wasn't allowing us to minister to any one else and tell him not to come back when I felt the Lord nudge me, "give him a chance, talk to him." So I did, I said, "what do you want in life Devin?" He answered, "I want to be a good father and husband, I want to be a businessman some day also." Then I asked him, "do you know any-one who is those things that you would want to be like?" He said "I want to be like you." So I told him, "if you want to be like me then get next to me and follow me, I won't let you down. Do what I say, do what I do, imitate me as I imitate Christ." "Follow me Devin, for two years and when you are done, I promise you'll like who you've become better than who you are now."

We have a thing at The Father's House called come to Jesus meetings with the pastor, and we identify this need by determining if your love tank is empty. So, over the next year Devin had more of these encounters than anyone else ever has. They are almost always about inappropriate action or disrespect towards a leader or in a meeting and we need to discuss the right thing to do.

Now Devin would be in total disbelief about this and say, "I couldn't be wrong but if you say it was wrong I will never do it again." In most cases he was true to his word, but in one area, submission to a young female leader, he just couldn't control himself. So we would meet. At the end of the first year when I offered him a second year of the first year internship he agreed and asked me why. I told him about his in-ability to follow and submit to that leader, that all of his problems in that year were about following her. When I offered him a third year of his first year internship, he also heard the same reason but I also asked him another question. I said, "Devin what are you going to say to me when I offer you your seventh and eighth go round on your first year?" He answered, "If that's what it takes I'm going to do it. But why do I have to do that?" The reason or answer that I had for him was that in every instance of getting in trouble in his life, it was the boss or the principal or the cops, never him. How many more good jobs did he want to lose or how many more leaders were going to give up on him like I almost did? His identity was what was screwed up, he had been told that his only reason for existing was to be a playmate for his older brother and he would tell everyone this.

It's been almost six years now, Devin has called me Pops since the conversation. He has achieved an amazing track record as my son. He was our children's pastor and the director of our food ministry. He also was a house leader in our drug and alcohol program. In short he has done everything that we have asked of him, followed our lead in every way, accepted discipline when needed. Devin recently married a girl from Ontario, Canada who had come to us from the school of ministry at the Toronto Airport Christian Fellowship. He is a son. He took to being parented, long after he should have received this training. He didn't get it when he was young, so who will give it to him now? If the church will step in to be fathers and mothers to people like Devin we will begin to see unbelievable results. Devin will be a world changer, he will affect many, he is a manuscript in progress and I can't wait to read the book titled Devin, the life and times of a son.

Then there is Louie, never told what to do or how to do it, he just figured it out as he went along. We met him when the head of Drug Court brought him to the leader of our Life Recovery Ministry in the middle of the night. Louie was going to go do something so that he could go back to jail. When the Drug Court employee saw him walking in the wrong neighborhood, she picked him up and brought him to us. In the first two weeks he did nothing but resist all authority and for the same reasons that Devin had. Authority figures were the ones who strip and cavity search you, they arrest you and take away your freedom.

The leader of his house complained to me daily about his argumentative and resistive nature and that he was disrupting the whole house. I was on my way to tell him to pack it up, just as he was having a revelation. A revelation that the leader, Andy (who was also an intern from TACF) had a life and there really wasn't any reason for him to be in Oroville except that he was there to give his life away for Louie. Louie went to Andy just before I arrived. He repented and thanked him for what he was trying to do. I didn't kick him out and he began to change. At the end of his year in LRM he applied for an internship. He was accepted and became a house leader. For the first time de began the process of submission to a father, it would have been far easier to receive the training when he was six or seven but I wasn't there then. I am now! He has become quite a man. On June second 2007 he married my daughter Nicole, who is the associate pastor of the Father's House Church and together they are the youth pastors, running a ministry called Fuzion.

Louie works for my construction company, which I hope to turn over to him one day when his transformation into a journeyman will be complete. He will be the father of my grandchildren and a member of my immediate family; he will be with us on holidays and vacations. Louie is a world changer and he is a son. He will make a difference to many as he gives his life away. Louie will be an inspiration to us all.

CHAPTER 5

A Ministry to the Addicted

THE MINISTRY to the addict is something that for years I thought was no problem. Just get them to experience the love of the Father through the outpouring of the Holy Spirit. When they have a profound touch from God then just begin to disciple them. I thought that people's lack of success was because they were not ready or not committed enough, they were choosing to lose. In 1997, we began to fast and prayer walk our city making declaration to God that if He would identify the harvest to us, we would be the workers that Jesus said were lacking. The Lord identified to us that the harvest was the dysfunctional people all over our city that couldn't be defined by addiction alone. Instead, they were lost and seemed to be unable, even with a revelation of God, to stop the current that continued to drag them toward destruction. We began to focus our church in the area of our city where the problem seemed to be the worst. We had a lot to learn about this ministry.

Here are some of the things that we have learned. First, is that the majority of these people desperately do not want to be who they have become. The second thing is that drug addiction is to dysfunction what a runny nose is to a cold. The problem that we define as drug addiction began in most people's lives very early on. Maybe even in the womb as an unwanted pregnancy and continued in abuse and rejection including abandonment. Most of these were born in unfair circumstances in what could easily be described as the toxic waste dumps of human life.

These beautiful children started out with all the promise that comes with being our Father's little ones. Soon after, maybe even in the womb they began to feel the effect of the careless things being said about them. Things about their gender or maybe that they are not wanted or how inconvenient their lives will be to their parents. Then upon entering this life they experience how much of an intrusion they are. They find themselves being mistreated, being called stupid, worthless, ugly, fat, lazy, told that they will never amount to anything. They begin the process of fulfilling these prophecies and the rebellion begins.

Very few people ever rebel by running from rejection, abuse and abandonment and turning to those things that are good for them. Instead, sex, drugs and eventually crime which leads to jail and legal problems then become a lifetime cycle.

In addition to this they have hoped to find the love that eluded them for all of their childhood. They look for love in all the wrong places practicing the principles that they were trained in, causing one disaster after another. Which includes having their own children, whom they vow will be different. They will not repeat the things that their parents did. This, they are completely unable to do. Then another little baby child is born and so the cycle continues.

We thank God for all the people who minister in jail and on the streets who love Jesus and have told our people about the love of the Father. This usually has the result of them reaching out for help.

Normally, this is how The Father's House Church finds them. They write or call us or they are brought to us by someone who wants to help them. Often they just walk in the front door of our services. It's no surprise to have many at the altar. They are tired and sorrowful and very repentant. They cry with the deepest emotion to the God of heaven and say, "please save me." They receive, experience and manifest the Lord's touch. They shout worship, and display clearly the "*he who is forgiven much loves much.*" They are exuberant, proclaiming undying love for God, even dancing in the revelation that since He has touched them with His presence and embraced them in a most powerful way, He has not rejected them. They cry first in deep grief, and then comes great joy. We take them into a residential program that we call Life Recovery Ministry where we isolate them to our campus. We drive them to job interviews, doctor's appointments, and court appearances. We feed them, teach them, love them, but most importantly we begin to father and mother them.

Now I wish that what I have described, the touch of God, the repentance and the program, that these would be the important part, But it has been proven to us over and over that these alone, do not work. It is impossible to reverse the effects of rejection and abandonment without the healing of the heart and the revelation of their father standing by them telling them that they are good and deserving, that they have value. Things that God the Father wants them to know. What we must not forget is that they need to know what not to do as well. Things parents should have taught them when they were young like how to deal with life when things don't go the way you want them to. If someone is unfair you don't throw the baby out with the bath water, you have to learn to deal with it. This is not the last unfair circumstance that you're going to face. Principles like this we learned at an early age but these ones didn't have that, so at 30, 40 and even 50 years old someone has to be the father and teach them how to live. If they never get fathered it is very difficult for them to relate to God as their Father. We see commonly in our church a steady flow of those who easily accept Jesus but mention the Father and you just get a blank stare. The Holy Spirit is cool, but tell them of the Father's love and they either don't understand or it's a bad thing. We must have in the church men who would be fathers to the fatherless and women who would be mothers. As well as young men and women who would round out the family and be brothers and sisters. It would have been great if more of our people grew up in functional families but they didn't. As a result, if the church family doesn't demonstrate to them the Father's love in practical, physical ways, then it will be very difficult to help them have a revelation of the Father's love.

The success in our ministry has been fantastic; we have seen so many cross over from dysfunction to sonship. These being the ones who begin to have a revelation of the Father's love for them. A wonderful bonus is that they become sons and daughters to our ministry and decide that they want to work in their Father's house, so they stay on as interns which we now have a staff of 31. These interns do the ministry to the children of our neighborhood who are also fatherless and to the youth, hoping to stop the cycle before they grow up. They do our homeless ministry and our outreach to the elder care facility. They work as well in our food bank and maintenance department. They give their lives away for the good of others which completes one of the most important transformations. They become givers as opposed to being takers, because all their lives they studied taking as if it were an art.

Now, anyone who has had one of our sons or daughters around them before they became children of the Father, can tell you they were takers. This is not what they wanted to be. So when introduced to giving, as it has been given to you, they go at it with all their hearts. They make fabulous sons and daughters, the best interns, and your church is much the richer with them worshiping with abandon, shouting their love. They repent deeply and emotionally for their sins. They laugh hard, cry hard and are very loving to their pastors.

The ministry to the addicted is the harvest that Jesus spoke of "*the harvest is plentiful but the workers are few.*" The job is not for a crusade or a weekend retreat, but it is for the long term. It has midnight phone calls and relapses and restarts, it has countless hours of teaching them principles and telling them what it is to be an adult. The job is for me fathering 30 or 40 people a day. A crash course in adulthood. The purpose in the end is them having a revelation of the Father's love.

I've been in ministry all my life, and never have I seen the kind of fruit that remains as I'm seeing now in the ministry to the addicted. So even if you only start with one addicted person that you know, maybe you can get a jump start on my learning curve. You need to understand that healing the heart and fathering increases the odds of them becoming sons of our Father one hundred percent. But don't forget that their free will cannot be violated and their poor choices are not your failure. Yet you will know it is worth it all if you see just one cross over to become a son, you will never be the same.

CHAPTER 6

Counting the Cost

JESUS SAID that, "*no builder builds a project without first sitting down to count the cost.*" Of course, in ministry if you could accurately know the cost, most of us would probably procrastinate the process until the opportunity passed us by. Yet there are some who could be like Jesus in the garden when he says, "*not my will but yours,*" when He already knew the cost of the project. Then He says in complete exhaustion "*it is finished.*" Then Jesus "*breathed his last.*"

You do not have to be in "the ministry to the poor" to relate to Jesus' example. Just be a person who gives your life away for the benefit of others and you will understand that you did not accurately count the cost at the first steps of your ministry. I do believe that it is important to know that ministry in most forms is a "*give and you shall receive*" proposition. That it usually is not over until you are ready to breathe your last. So far I have not breathed my last and neither has my wife. We continue to give our lives away.

The cost has been that we have spent all 30 years of our married life pursuing the Lord's work. Which means laying down our lives for our brothers and sisters. Laying down our lives was a beautiful idea that sounded great which we thought translated into being honored and elevated to a celebrity status if you are successful. You see we were caught up in the definition of success being large numbers showing up, although that was not on our minds at the time. I must confess that this is always a pressure to young people in ministry since it seems that only those with large numbers are ever celebrated.

One of the first things that the Lord had to re-teach us about counting the cost was that he did not call us as shepherds to count the sheep. He called us to love the sheep. Since we knew His words about, *"no greater love"* and being *"the servant of all,"* it was time to re-define the meaning of success in ministry to **giving your life away for the life of another.** So, the first cost we had to count in starting the ministry to this poor community was the cost of our lives. We had to ask, is it worth our lives?

The second cost to consider was, is it worth our children's lives? Our children were 16, 15, 11 and 7 when we started bringing them with us to this neighborhood. They had never seen anything like this before. Our kids probably wondered what they had done wrong to deserve this. They were not treated well and they were not used to this. There also was danger all around us and they were not used to that either. Not only were there social differences in the way people lived but also in the definition of right and wrong. In some cases, there was no right and wrong, only what can be taken advantage of. Our children were not used to that either.

It has been 11 years and we believe that spending so much time in Southside has greatly enhanced our children's view of ministry. They could not possibly have the same mistaken view of success that we had, nor will they spend so much of their adult lives learning these lessons since they learned them growing up. They truly have given their lives away for the benefit of others and shown the *"no greater love"* to their brothers and sisters. We recently asked each of our sons and daughters if they ever felt robbed or injured by our commitment to ministry and each answered the same, "sharing us with so many got to be a burden from time to time," "I get tired of everyone's expectations of me" and "its like living in a fish bowl." One of my daughters still says things like, "let's not talk about the church all night tonight." The good thing is that should any of them decide to go into a ministry they will have understood that there are costs that must be counted before beginning.

CHAPTER 7

The Investment in Dollars and Sense

THE THIRD cost I would think should have been the first is the cost in money. However, this list is a list based on value, and money certainly comes after the two others as values.

At the beginning of our life together I explained to Vicki about giving and how I gave 10 percent off of the top of my pay. She thought that this was strange and probably would not be doing anything like this. You see, we met when I was 15 and she was 14 years old through mutual cousins. We lived a whole country apart, her in Chicago and me in California. Other than at weddings for those cousins, we wrote and talked on the phone on and off for seven years. In 1975, some three years later, I met the Lord and was writing her about Jesus. She thought that I was wearing pink togas and selling flowers in airports, so she did not take me too serious.

On a visit to her in 1979, she prayed to receive Jesus and two months later we were getting married! By the time we had the talk about money we were days away from our wedding day. When I learned how she felt about giving I just began to tithe for her. I listened to her say what she made and how many hours that she worked and I gave based on the total of both of our incomes. Our finances were divinely blessed, which when compared to her way of giving was very convincing to her. She became a true believer in giving and to this day has become the most generous person I've ever known. God began to challenge us in his Word, and also to our hearts. We soon were giving twenty percent, then thirty percent. We began to talk about what it would be like to give ninety percent. Asking questions like, is it possible? Could we be so blessed? How do you do this? Well the first answer is, just be in ministry. Those given over to the ministry will at this time nod their heads and chuckle. For Vicki and I it began to be obvious that the Lord was testing us and equipping us for something in our future. We did not count the cost at this time but instead just paid it. It did not always make 'sense', we had to just trust.

CHAPTER 8

The Call to Start
The Father's House

WHEN THE call to start The Father's House Church came we needed to count the cost. To Vicki and I the cost was our lives and our children's lives, and we prayed about this money thing, (the mystery of Christianity.) Here is what God has shown me. First, He asked me where I got the idea of ten percent giving and the rest belongs to me? I told him from Malachi. He then asked if I believed that I should live under the new covenant or the old covenant? I said "the new." Next began a bible study on giving and monetary stewardship, to show me the answer to the question, what is the cost?

I looked at the parable of the talents and saw how much was required of each guy. It was all of it, the investment and the increase was given to the master, all of it. Then I looked at the story of the widow's mite, was she honored for her gift or the fact that by giving her two mites she was giving her all? In the story of the rich young ruler, he received an answer to his question about getting to heaven, he was told that he still lacked one thing, "*sell all that you have and give it to the poor*". I was pretty sure this story was not in the New Testament to say that he was the only one in history who might need to get free of his possessions and give all.

Jesus turned to his disciples and said, "*sell your possessions and give the money to the poor. You can't serve two masters, where your treasure is there will your heart be also, why do you store up treasure on earth where moth and rust consume, it is better to store your treasure in heaven where moth and rust does not consume. It is harder for a rich man to get to heaven than for a camel to get through the eye of a needle.*" If I want to get rich and get to heaven, what are my odds? They are the same as getting that camel through the eye of that needle. Okay it's time for a new plan. My plan must include not possessing wealth but managing it for the kingdom. The church in The Book of Acts understood this. In fact there is continual references by Jesus throughout the Gospels and constant examples of His position on what actions with money are seen as faith.

If you were to read the Gospels with a note pad and journalled every time Jesus talked about or gave examples about giving, you would be astounded by the overwhelming facts about Jesus' teaching. Some of you would probably wonder how you came to believe what you believe, when the evidence demands a different verdict or understanding than you have operated under. Even the one boy who planned ahead and brought the two fish and five loaves gave them all. For a moment he was without them and hungry. If he had not given them he probably would have still seen a miracle, but he would not have been a miracle. He would not be in the Bible and when we get to heaven and you meet him and he said I am the boy with the loaves and fishes, you would say, Who? Instead, he's the boy who planned ahead and saved up for later when he would be hungry. When the time did come and he was hungry, **he did not give a tithe, he gave all.** Now when we meet him and he describes who he is, we will know exactly who he is. He is the boy who allowed himself to be a miracle and to participate in a miracle of Jesus. He did receive an all you can eat meal with a doggie bag to go, more important is that he is spoken of with honor in every Christian church in the world and you will know him in eternity. Selflessness always produces an eternal result. Jesus taught that even a cup of water given to a little or lesser one would not go unrewarded.

I will just suggest the above exercise with the Holy Spirit's guidance. Read the New Testament seeking an understanding of the cost of a Jesus type ministry to the poor and the lost that surround you. Journal as you read, and come to a Holy Spirit led understanding of the cost. I have found no other example in the New Testament than **ALL**.

My understanding got brighter when the vision of the church was directed to a property that had an extra lot next door. The day we saw it on a prayer walk, my visionary gifting had a field day and I saw the new church in a house. I bought the property and designed a house with a 34'x34' living room to house the church. We could grow to 100 people in this house. We began and the project went to the point of the foundation being set up. Then the project stopped for a time, because of the lack of money. This was frustrating and I felt like it was a failure of my leadership. Why couldn't I get this done? Lord didn't you show me this vision? I even saw the exact building in my vision. I said, "You know Lord that to know Your will is to know my future". Then to quote again my good friend Forrest, "GOD SHOWED UP" and I will never be the same.

Now to quote another good friend of mine Psalty The Singing Songbook I said, "IS THAT YOU LORD?" The Lord said, "Yes it's Me".

CHAPTER 9

The Revelation of Cost

I WAS sitting on the stoop of the house on that property, looking at this foundation when God showed up. He said, "Steve why have you not done what I showed you to do?" I answered, (as is wise to do when God shows up and uses your name), "because there is no money to go any farther."

He said unexpectedly, "do you really want to stand before me to explain that the people of Southside could not have the church that I birthed in you, because of your need to provide for your own future? Do you want me to tell you then, why you never saw the completion of the visions that I showed you?" I must tell you that conversations like this don't happen very often in my life, it takes me a minute to catch up with Him.

You see He did not talk to me in the wavelength that I had been pondering. In other words I was thinking about my failure, but not in the same way that He was referring to, my thinking went something like this: Why can't I get this done? Also, why is this my gig? He's God, it's his plan. If He really wanted this done He would provide for it. It's usually at this time, just when I am blaming Him that I have these actual conversation or revelations of a lifetime.

Just when I am sitting there trying to figure out what I am hearing, like what providing for my own future means, and is it possible for me to cancel out his plan for me, I get this vision of a bank account, one with a good amount of money in it. Then I realize, it's my retirement account. Just when I realize what account it is He says, "Do you really want only what you can provide for yourself? Or do you want to be like the lilies of the field, not worrying about what you will wear and what you will eat. Does worrying about today instead of tomorrow and letting tomorrow worry about itself seem good to you?" Like Job I said, "I have spoken and I will now listen, if you will speak I will do what you say." He began, *"if anyone would come after me let him first deny himself, pick up his cross and follow me. The Son of man has nowhere to lay his head, and why do you worry about what you will eat and what you will wear, consider the lilies of the field, they neither toil nor spin. Yet Solomon in all of his glory, is he not clothed as beautifully, would not your Father in heaven also care for you?"*

Why did I have this retirement account I asked myself? It was actually a requirement of one of my church positions. To prove that I was a good steward, a good husband and father. Also, every speaker and book on the subject says it in a way that would make a person look unrighteous or unholy if you did not have one. The pressure is immense to plan for the future. It tempts us to have life insurance to make sure that our loved ones will eat and sleep in case God does not provide. To plan for the future is the very definition of good steward-ship. These words I have quoted from Jesus must be considered. The Lord said one last thing to me on that stoop, *"when I return, will I find any faith left on the earth?"*

I fell to the ground to repent and thank Him for waking me from my slumber. I begged Him for the courage to live according to His word. I got up and went to find my wife. When I got finished explaining to her what God had shown me she had a very concerned look on her face and said, "I don't think that I am on your page on this one."

When she left, I repented and asked God if He could undo what I had done to her. You see it was me who taught her about trusting in retirement accounts, life insurance, paychecks and companies and even the economies of the world. It was me who led her to a position of faith in something other than God. I was the one, and I needed forgiveness and rescue. I prayed, "please undo what I have caused in her, let her please You in financial matters and live by faith again."

Our retirement account is half hers and half mine. About seven days went by and I hoped to sit down for another try at coming to an agreement with Vicki. Then, my office manager asked what this check from the retirement account was for? Vicki, had called them on the day that I had talked to her, because she also felt the incredible nature of this truth of God's word. She wanted to do it before fear had a chance to stop her. So, I called also, and cashed out my half, it had to be done over the loud objections of the financial planner. He still wants to tell me about the return that I would have had, but I always tell him to come visit The Father's House and see the fruit of that investment, this is my return.

The children that have been rescued, the youth, the food lines that form and the people who come to that building to get fed. The old ones who have prayed to receive Jesus just before they died in New Hope Ministries, which is housed in that building. The 1000 meals a month prepared in that kitchen and fed to the staff and clients of Life Recovery Ministry, which is rescuing the addicted in our city. Taking people over from trusting in religion and church and bringing them to wholeness. The Christmas programs and back to school backpack programs, not to forget the mentoring and tutoring. We have a dream come true school of ministry that started in that building and is now our intern school and ministry apprenticeship.

There is Vicki my wife, the person who trusted the Lord for her future, and invested her faith in the building. She does healing the heart prayer and counseling, helping people get free from the wounds of their past. Yet, the investment advisor wants me to consider the monetary gain that I would have realized. When compared to just one truth, that *"without faith it is impossible to please God"* not even considering the soul harvest, just the faith harvest, there is no return on investment that could compare!

Yes, there is a cost, in term of monetary investment. God has shown me that it was not ever His intention that I settle for the blessings that return to me from a 10 percent tithe. It was always his will that I receive the abundant blessings, given to those who give all.

There have been hundreds of miracles of a financial nature in the Father's House Church, but finances have been the greatest struggle on a daily basis, greater than any other struggle. We built businesses to support the work. When you are successful in ministry to the unchurched children, youth and adults of your city, they do not know how to give, nor do they have anything to give. When they do learn to give, the ALL does not add up to enough to pay the bills. So we began to build a structure of supply. We had a construction company which provided jobs to the people. This increased their giving, plus the profits from that company were substantial and built most of the infrastructure of the church. We also developed a real estate company that was very successful. In fact, it gave 100 percent of its earnings to the church. We loved this process; it was a win, win proposition.

In June of 2005 the housing market began to slow down. The effect on the income of the church was to the extent that we could no longer maintain the level of service to the youth and children. We were in the homes of 287 children per week doing in-person visits. This in addition to our pick up routes for weekly services had to stop. This is just an example of the slow down, it had much more effect than I can describe. A more revealing circumstance is that Vicki and I had felt that the support of the Father's House was our job. We didn't just want to support it, we felt that God had made it our job. The stress became huge. Just when our income was down to almost nothing we began to feel that the Lord was telling us that He was changing our assignment, that it was not our job any longer. I did not accept this without some confirmation. Vicki and I were not hearing the same.

I had been told many times that it was not my job; it was the Lord's job, by many well-meaning friends. I said that there was no way that I could fail to give to cover the staff and interns who were giving their lives away. Plus, the people of the church were not giving what they had been and the situation just got worse. At about this time a team came from Restoring the Foundations ministries to take our entire staff through their deliverance ministry and healing process. One of their trainers came to us having asked all of her intercessors and prophetic contacts to pray for a couple that she was taking through the ministry. She asked them to let her know what the Lord was saying. What the Lord was saying shocked us both! This woman did not know anything about our struggle to know the will of God concerning the finances. Here's what she said, "there were many different words but the one that seemed to be repeated was this, you are tied to a rock and you have been pulling it up this hill. People have been telling you that it is not your job to pull that rock up that hill. But you keep saying, no God told me to pull this rock up this hill and I am not going to stop." Then she continued, "The Lord says that He did tell you that, and He is proud of you for not giving up, now He is cutting the rope and you will run up the hill, and when you get there the rock will be there. It is not your job to carry the rock any more."

In the two years since this word we have not been able to support the work of the church. Our personal finances have been a challenge to understand. The church has survived and grown tremendously. On the other hand, we have come to the brink of personal bankruptcy. I have had the hardest times of my life, trying to understand what is going on.

Then on New Year's day I was awakened by the Lord and led to drive to every property that we owned. I spoke over these properties and said, "this property belongs to my Father, every rock and tree". If it was a house then I would say "every part and piece is the Lord's and if He wants someone else to own it, then bless His holy name."

It caused so much peace and released Vicki and I from the burden of ownership. Our trust is not in homes or economies, it is in the Lord and the knowledge that He loves us. With property or not, with our reputation or not, our best asset is His power and presence in our lives.

The ministry miracles continue to increase and the ministries that operate out of The Father's House just continue to be birthed, with good leadership and people getting the chance to be used by the Lord.

When I look at the circumstances of my situation I can really get frustrated and even mad, sometimes coming very close to shouting out at the Lord. This I don't recommend, yet when the creditors are calling daily and many friends in the construction industry are hurting because of your situation, it happens.

This is where I found myself one day in a weakened state and I asked the Lord if this was the reward for faithfulness? I knew immediately that I had made myself out to be righteous and the Lord out to be unrighteous. This again, brought about a conversation opportunity between the Lord and me. He began asking me "how much money did I think that I had given away in the last ten years?" I thought about it for moment and knew the amount. Then He asked me "how much money had I made in the last ten years?" Again, I thought about it and as the number was coming to mind I realized that what I had given and what I had made was the same number. I said to the Lord in stunned awe, "how is this possible?" He did not answer my specific question, He just asked me how many properties we had acquired with no money for the down payment? Again, I did not know the answer but a number came to mind, seventy. As I was pondering this fact and coming to the conclusion that it was about right, He asked me, "have you known one thousand people who had tithed?" I had, so I said, "I am sure that I have known that many people who have tithed." He asked me, "has even one of them testified that I am not faithful?" "No Lord, not even one," I said. "Then if not one person who tithes says that I am unfaithful, would I not be faithful to someone who gives their all?" He asked. "Then what the heck is going on in my finances?" I asked. A verse in Job came to mind right then, *"when you have been tested you will come forth as gold."* At first the most amazing thing was that I didn't realize what we had done, I didn't realize we had given such a high percentage of our income. Then I was overjoyed to know that it was a test. I know what the testing of my faith brings to me! I want it all!

The next revelation that came to me was that I was not helping the church financially and it was more fruitful than ever, it had not failed. It is much better being tested, as compared to failing, or feeling that God might be mad at you. Being tested can come with peace. It is a peace that can't be explained, or at least *"passes understanding,"* plus it really does *"rule in your heart."* Just to know that He is aware of your situation and has a plan for you, this is good. I know that I should have known this but when you expect your faith to have a certain outcome and things don't work out the way that you planned, it is easy to begin to really feel pressure.

The cost; I am glad that I did not know how hard it would be. Looking back I would not change a thing. I am willing to spend more and yes even **all**. The cost is not so hard to describe looking back, it is the fruit that is unbelievable. You would have to see the growth in the workers, that only a short time ago they were the fruit. Yes, *"some do trust in chariot and horses,"* and some in construction companies and real estate offices. Still others trust in savings accounts and retirement portfolios. God is teaching Vicki and I along with about three or four hundred of our closest friends to trust completely in the name of the Lord. I must believe, even if it is hard, that Jesus is *"building his church and the gates of hell will not prevail against it."*

There are other costs in this ministry. I would like to just touch on one more, the cost to your heart. Not the beating organ in your chest, but the cost to your willingness to love.

A friend of mine that I have loved and valued for four or five years now, told me over and over again that it is difficult for someone like me to understand drug addicts. He said, "they will break your heart. Only someone very strong in what they believe will not eventually give up." He was right, if you do this ministry to the addicted, or the poorer communities, the weight of your disappointment will become very hard to bear. If you do it unto the Lord, you will be satisfied. You will know that the word of God never returns to him without completing its purpose. You teach them the truth and they choose, there are no robot disciples. Live a life in front of them that is a light in the world, a standard to rally around, give them fruit to inspect and show them the heart of the Father. Live a life that they could imitate and follow. Then leave the rest in the hands of God who loves them more than you do! The outcome is not the proving of the ministry's success, nor is it a sign of its failure.

A few years ago God put a man in my life that I built houses for. It was a project of about ten homes and we spent a lot of time on it. As I got to know him I learned that he was a combat veteran of the Vietnam War and I also became aware that he had a severe alcohol and prescription medicine problem.

One day he got very sick and went to the doctor, only to find out that he was terminally ill with cancer. It only took a couple of weeks until he was on his deathbed where I pleaded with him to receive Jesus. He refused to the end, his last intelligible words were a loud "NO" and then he became delirious. My friend soon passed on and for a few minutes I felt that I somehow failed him. "THEN GOD SHOWED UP." He showed me how much He loved this man, how He had tried to reach him in Vietnam, but my friend had been mad at him. God showed me how He had loved him to the end by sending him someone who would get it right and tell him about the mercy of the God who loved him. It was his choice, everyone has them and their choices do not determine my success or God's. Jesus did not fail my friend, and neither did I.

He had answered the call of the U.S. government and gone to West Point Military Academy. My friend had believed the words of the politicians. When he got to the war, his idealism failed him, his commanders failed him, his training even failed him. Last, but not least when he got home, his country failed him. He somehow decided that a God who would let him suffer the consequences of his own actions was the one to blame, and that by rejecting His love somehow my friend was getting back at God. He blamed God. I was a witness, and with great pride I watched God chase him to the last breath. I had told him, that in just a few minutes, he would be in the presence of the Lord, and that he would want to stay in His presence. "Just call out to him," I said. A man who has faced war, been through so many very difficult tests in life, couldn't do this simple thing because he was mad at God.

The cost of this ministry, the cost to our heart can cause burnout. Ministering to unfaithful, accusational, procrastinating, weak-minded people who choose not to listen to you can cause burnout. Burnout seems to be the greatest cause of ministry failure. Which we take to our hearts as our failure. People's failures seem to be the greatest cause of burnout. One can find it difficult to believe that God does not take away a person's right to fail. They get to choose. Success would be nothing if one could not fail, God did not take their ability to fail away. Burnout would be a thing of the past if we would remember that their inability to accept God's love and mercy is not the measure of a fruitful ministry, that their failure is their choice. I must show them the good in God, the love of the Father; the rest is their choice.

This truth is the pathway to freedom from this cost. Yet someone with any heartbeat at all will struggle, at times even suffer, from the loss of someone who you have laid down your life for.

Remember this, Jesus laid down His life for them, it is His will that none should perish, He gave them free will and choice. In the end, He will let them go. He will say, "*I knew you not.*" We must cherish the calling and gifting that God has given to us, using them well, giving our ALL and resting in the peace of God.

CHAPTER 10

The Benefit Package

THE BENEFIT package? Now I know that some of you are scratching your head about now because you think that you have never had one of these benefit packages. But I am talking about the benefits of the ministry to the poor, the people, who thank you for saving their lives. They tell you that without you they would be dead. If you had not helped them identify the times in their lives when they were wounded, they never would have gotten free. Plus the benefit of the interns whose horizons are expanding, beyond even my imagination, and I have quite an imagination; they dream about the opportunities in which they can give their lives away. They give their lives now, serving in ministry. They are already changing the world for others. The benefits that I am referring to is the benefits of being used by God to rescue people who are trapped in misery and want out.

People who have suffered, some for many years, like Bob. He has been a severe alcoholic for many years, 40 I believe. Bob came to us looking like death. An old friend of his brought him to us and paid his first month's program fees. His friend also gave him a job so that we would keep him under our wing day and night. Bob began to tell me stories in his talks with me. He was a Vietnam veteran, and a former prisoner of war. This decorated veteran was to say the least, a fighter.

In LRM Bob noticed that the men in his house were watching a movie called Apocalypse Now. In this movie, there is real war footage of swift boats on the river, and when shooting breaks out they show footage of a gunner on the front of the boat. Bob said, "that's me on the gun." They played it back and forth trying to get a glimpse of the man sitting next to them.

Veterans of Vietnam don't normally talk about the war. Watching this movie caused our conversations to open up about his experience. The first thing Bob wanted me to know was how much he hated some people. I don't mean the word hate, I mean murder hate, blood in the eyes hate. Of course he hated the Vietcong who tortured him for eighteen months as a P.O.W., starving him, beating him, and using psychological torture. Whew, it's no wonder he hated so much.

I began to understand and admire this broken soul. He was without his booze and I thought he would die from the stress of it. He could not go numb without his booze. He would shout with vile contempt at a famous actress whose words the Vietcong had used to torture him as they said, "she was only saying what everyone was saying back home." In forty years he has turned her into much more of a villain than she was.

His hate was devastating. His stories continued about a young lieutenant, a son of someone important whose privilege Bob felt was why he had been captured. Bob was not ready to forgive. These talks stirred up his hate; he would cry then rant in profanities. Up, then down, relapse, cry for help, just miserable.

I was sure that God could help him. Bob would not give in, he would not relent, the force of his life that caused him to survive Vietnam also caused him to resist in the most miserable situation of one's soul that I had ever seen. We seemed helpless to bring him to the table, he trusted no one. Again, just when the situation appeared to be at it's worst, as Forrest Gump would say, "GOD SHOWED UP," and this is what He did.

I saw Bob at a local restaurant with the foreman of his company, a very good man who also wanted to help Bob. We talked as we walked to our cars then Bob went off. He cussed me, told me that I was worthless, he told me where to put my ministry and how lucky I was he didn't kick my rear. All the while his foreman and I are standing there with our mouths wide open amazed. I told him to go home and pack his stuff and put it by the door until we had a meeting. No, "I'm out of here" he told me. I was sad, I felt this warrior, this man's man, with strength beyond imagination was lost to me, lost to my ministry. I hoped that he could find another person like me out there, one that could see him, the real man. I prayed for Bob in my truck as I left the parking lot. A few minutes later my phone rang, it was Bob's foreman. He asked if Bob could talk to me. He had told Bob that his job was on the line. The foreman told Bob that if he left the ministry, he would fire him, (even if he did not fire him now) he reminded Bob that he was not employable when drinking.

Bob got on the phone asking if he could stay and would I come talk to him. I did, the Lord was with me and I went hoping to free this prisoner, still captive forty-some years after his bloody, life saving escape from the Vietcong.

We sat at a table in the house where Bob lived in the program. He began to tell me about a little girl that he had adopted in Vietnam. He took her in because he had killed a sniper who had their boat pinned down and when they approached the body of the sniper, it was a woman with a little girl in a pouch in front of her. This baby had perished with her mother. Next to her on the ground was another little girl about three years old. Bob would not leave her to certain death. This was beginning of the life of guilt and shame which began with the killing of his enemy. He took this three year old little girl to live with him. Each time he saw this little girl he was reminded of how her mother and sister had perished at his hand.

One day when his boat was not up on duty, they received a call to go and pick up a patrol upriver. The young officer of privilege that he hated so much was supposed to be on duty, it was his patrol. The radioman said that this young lieutenant had refused, yet this patrol needed to be picked up. So Bob's commander took the assignment and went upriver and since it was an unscheduled trip he could not find anyone to watch her, so he took the little girl with him.

They were ambushed by three formerly US P.T. boats that had been given to the Vietcong by Cambodia. In a terrible firefight they lost their boat and all hands including his little girl. Bob loved her and yet he could not save her. Bob was floating in the river wounded, the only survivor. He surrendered, all was lost.

Bob tells that he was tied to a tree and mistreated for eighteen months. One day when all the captives were sure that they would die of starvation, one of them said they should pray. In a desperate plea they prayed, Bob says that at that exact second a snake fell out of that tree right at their feet. They ate the snake. These men tried to escape, most were killed, Bob was shot several times, yet he got away. Bob survived and it has been more than forty years of hating. He hated the actress, the politician who was the officer of privilege, the President who sold the P.T. boats to Cambodia, plus the Vietcong and the war protesters who called him names when he came home.

I asked him if he was ready to forgive. The officer of privilege had recently run for President and had used his decorations as bragging rights for why he deserved to be President. Bob was not ready to face this yet, so he changed the subject.

Bob told me that he had been to the doctor; he was told that he had cancer and the doctor wanted to treat it. The description of his treatment was not pretty. He asked me a question that I had never been asked. I was glad that God was there to give me the answer. Bob said, "Steve, do you think it would be all right if I told them no treatment and just lived as long as I can, then just die?" I answered, "I do not have a problem with a man accepting death as long as he has peace about the next life."

I also told him that he did not have a relationship with God that had born any fruit. He did not respond to that. He only heard that I was okay with him dying.

Then he asked if there was any possibility that he could see that little girl again? I answered, "I am not the judge but I think that she will be with the Father, so if you are going to see her again, you should work on making sure you accept the plan that God made for you." "How" he asked? "Forgiveness, yours and the people that you hate, the rest is easy." We tried to pray him through forgiving these people but he just couldn't get anywhere.

Under my breath, I asked the Lord for help, just then I had a word from the Lord, "he cannot surrender." I understood, he had surrendered before, to the Vietcong and that didn't work out so well for him. I told him what I had heard the Lord say and I told him that he could trust the Lord. I asked Bob if he had ever made a vow not to ever surrender again, Bob answered with fire in his eyes, "I said never, they'll have to kill me." "Well you can trust God, you can surrender to Him," I said. With great fear in his eyes he said, "I'll do whatever you tell me Steve." "God is here Bob, surrender to Him." Bob lifted his hands over his head with an imaginary M-16 rifle in his hands just like a soldier would surrender. He told the Lord that he would surrender, emotions started to flow.

Picture this proud man of war, straight back, powerful hands, surrendering to the Lord for the first time in his life. Surrendering to the Lord just like he had surrendered to the Vietcong forty years earlier. In Bob's mind he was risking being tortured again for the chance at being set free. I do not believe that I have ever been more proud to serve God in ministry than at that moment.

Our Father chased Bob for forty years and cornered him at that table and he surrendered. Bob had given his "last full measure" to quote Abraham Lincoln. He had died many deaths in Vietnam yet he lived to suffer another day, and forty years more. Then God reached him!

"Now are you ready to forgive?" I asked. "Yes I will try," he replied. We began, Bob forgave the lieutenant, he forgave the actress. Bob forgave the president who gave the P.T. Boats to Cambodia, he forgave the protestors who called him a baby killer, Bob forgave everyone, including God. He was healed of cancer at that table. Later, because he was so impressed with the cancer cure he asked for prayer for a blood disease and was healed!

What a great testimony he has become. If Bob had not blown his cork at me or the lieutenant had not run for President or his foreman had not gotten him back to the house to call me, I don't know if I would have gotten this opportunity.

Our Father would have still chased Bob all the way. I love Bob, I love Jesus, and He uses me as his tool to accomplish His will. What vacation pay, health insurance, dental plan, retirement fund, or promotion could compare to the benefit package that comes with just giving all to the Lord and delighting in his ministry?

CHAPTER 11

The Benefit of all Benefits

"ARE YOU the one"? John's disciples asked Jesus. Jesus answered with a list of signs. One of the signs that Jesus said would answer John's question was to tell him that the "gospel is preached to the poor". The evidence that the Messiah has come is that the gospel is preached to the poor. The poor have good news and not by accident, this was deliberate. The benefit of having the Messiah in your midst is worth any cost or investment of life that it takes to have Him present.

Moses saw a peculiar thing, a bush was on fire but not burning. He turned aside to see this thing and he had a face to face encounter with God. God told Moses to go get His people away from the most powerful king in the world of men.

Moses had been raised with this king and knew that he was ruthless. "*Who should I tell him sent me?*" This seems to me like a reasonable question. God says *"tell him that I AM sent you."* *"Who?"* Moses asked, *"I AM THAT I AM"* God replied. Now in English this looks like the meaning is, tell him that I exist, or I exist that I exist. If this is the whole meaning then people would say, I hope so but it is said of every god that they exist. Every believer, in every god, says that their god exists. I want to know more about this name, this cannot be all that He meant by this phrase.

I can imagine that Moses wants Pharaoh to know more than that He exists if he's going to return to Egypt. He needs a God that is with him and he needs Pharaoh to know it. So as you look into this word I AM, you begin to understand that God is saying, tell them I AM PRESENT THAT I AM PRESENT or I AM WITH YOU AND I AM WITH YOU. The greatest miracle in this story as I see it, is the fact that God's presence is with him. God even said to Moses that this was His name. He wanted to be known as the One who is with him. Moses didn't go alone, the one who is "present" was with him. Facing Pharaoh would be much easier with God present with you.

Long before I believed that Jesus was real, I knew that something was. The awe that you feel at the ocean or the Grand Canyon, or as a child looking at the stars. The mystery of it all screams out that somebody is there. Then people just make something up and worship the stars or something else, they create God in their own image.

God says to Moses, *"I am the one who is present."* This presence makes Him awesome but I think that He meant even more than this. I believe He means "I AM THE ONE WHO IS PRESENT IN YOUR MIDST," is present with you. Now you're talking, it makes sense to me now that a single individual who knows the Pharaoh would go back across this deadliest of all deserts to rescue a people that used to be his slaves. Moses had a close encounter with God and he was forever changed. That encounter ended with Moses knowing that God would go with him. The great big wonderful secret he had that the Pharaoh was about to learn was that his daddy could really beat up the Pharaoh's daddy.

Moses was not alone, He who was with him was greater than

all of them that would be against him. It is great that God is in the world and that is how we get these Rocky Mountains and Niagara Falls but can you imagine what is possible to a man or woman that has God present with them? Think of the wonders that would follow such a person. Sickness and disease in complete submission, the evil spirits crying out for him begging, *"have mercy on us."* The sea would part and make way for that person. The mercy that would be shown to the poor in spirit like skin disease and deformities being healed, prostitutes finding value in themselves and being made new. Everyone who *"seeks finds"* and *"everyone who knocks, the doors are open to them."*

What does a world look like when THE GOD WHO IS PRESENT IN YOUR MIDST, makes Himself known, and is going with you to free people? What is possible to a man who would believe this?

This God who is present, presents a problem if people will not live a holy and obedient life. He is a jealous God. Ask Uzza, a young man that is described as a man whose character is pretty good, the "presence" of the "presence" cost him his life. Ask a hundred and thirty thousand Israelites who tried to make a graven image of that presence. How about the Philistines and their hemorrhoids when they thought they would entertain the "presence" in their towns and cities. God told the priest to be careful not to desecrate the Ark of the Covenant, or they would surely die.

Then He does a most interesting thing, He becomes flesh and dwells among us, born of the flesh. Wow! The presence of God in the flesh of a man! Considering God's past record regarding protecting His presence, I would say that this is a drastic measure. Have you ever thought about this before? When Jesus was teaching at the end of his time on earth, He gives the disciples instructions that they should do nothing but wait on the Holy Spirit. He then says something so bizarre, given the historical record of the protection of His presence, he says, *"My Father and I will come and make our home in you."*

"Home in you"? That is what He said. I had thought that Jesus dying for unrighteous people was a miracle. Then I considered this,

God who is Holy, living in man who is sinful, this is miraculous. He was then, in Moses' day, and He is now in my day, the GOD WHO IS PRESENT IN OUR MIDST. What midst do I want Him in? Me, I want Him in me, just as He promised. If I could learn to live in just one of His promises it would be this, the Father and Son in me and going with me and all that this means.

He also said, "*where two or more are gathered in my name, there will I be.*" How about His promise to be, "*mighty in the midst of thee,*" and "*I will inhabit the praises of my people,*" I want Him in these midst's as well. If I only had time to get one thing right in my life of living and loving Jesus, it would be the understanding of what a man can do who understands God in our midst, or the God who is THE PRESENT ONE.

I think the evidence here that calls for a verdict is that having God in your midst is definitely a very good thing and probably the most important benefit to be valued.

David seems to have come to this conclusion when he wrote the Psalms because they are full of the wonder of God's touch and feel. David knew that the eyes of the Lord were upon him and he longed to see the days that we have before us and take for granted. He sang praises to God while alone in a field or just sitting with the King and it was soothing to the soul because this presence of God inhabited these praises. God is drawn to the love of his people and should be worshiped by anyone who has actually met Him. David understood the benefits of having the presence of God with him, so he set up a worship tabernacle where music was played. God was worshiped 24 hrs a day for 36 years non stop, what better way is there to have God's presence in your city?

David and Moses had access to wonderful manifestations of the Father's presence. Yet they longed for the day that we live in. Their experience with THE PRESENT ONE was one of an external God who lived around them and was with them as a friend or master.

Jesus gave us Christians something so much better, the baptism of the Holy Spirit. God inhabiting us to allow us to become sons as we are bathed in the presence of His holiness. I did not understand this when I said, "Jesus come into my heart and be my Lord and Savior." How could I have understood the awe and wonder of this benefit?

All you have to do is trade in one mortal life that was not that good. Then receive God into your heart who said that His name is, "*I AM THAT I AM,*" the one who is present in your midst or present with you. When looking at the benefits of being in the ministry of Jesus don't forget this one, being the home of the Father and the Son, the dwelling place of his Holy Spirit.

The evidence of the presence of the Messiah was, as Jesus said, "*the blind are healed, lepers are cleansed, and the gospel is preached to the poor.*" In the ministry to the poor we should expect this to be the minimum outcome of our faith.

As Christians the presence of the Messiah is not just with us but in us and the minimum expectation should be the greatest benefit, the evidence of His presence in us.

The Lord is present in us, what comes with Him is incredible. Read about heaven, or Christian living in the epistles and the book of Acts, then read the promises of Jesus about what to expect as a believer. Heaven here or in the next life are heavenly because He is there. When you pray, "*let Your kingdom come let Your will be done, here as it is in heaven*" what you want is Jesus, here in you, just as He is in heaven. Jesus is the benefit, turn aside to see this peculiar thing. Seek His presence and you will find Him. He is knocking on the door of your heart, your church, your business and he is not casual, He wants in. Since the beginning He has declared, "*I AM THAT I AM.*"

CHAPTER 12

The Fruit

WE STARTED out as a church seeking to identify the harvest that was ready, and then to be the workers. I had been a youth pastor for many years. In those many years I had heard many times in churches the question asked, at what age did you first come to a belief in Jesus? The answer always was that 80% or more were under 18 yrs. old when they met Jesus. Yet churches rarely spent 5% of their budget on this age group. They usually spent 95% or more on the 20% harvest. Now this is because the majority of the people in their church are over 18 yrs. old and they give 99% of the money. It does tend to be short sighted on the outreach part because, if people in church are having less kids than in past generations then the numbers will begin to reverse themselves and then future adults in church giving the 99% will begin to dwindle and even though the number 99% is the same, it will be 99% of a lower gross number.

Anyways if you're still with me, we wanted to go after the 80%

harvest and we did. We began to do morning prayer walks around the local high schools and established a children's ministry fashioned after Sidewalk Sunday School programs that we had sent interns to. Our daughter Nicole and our first intern Lisa, both freshly retuned from the School of Ministry in Toronto, Canada, began a program called Saturday Sunday School and did pick up routes and designed a most miraculous ministry to the children of Oroville. The children enjoy songs, and skits with repeat characters that they love, lots of rewards and prizes for learning, and prizes for listening. The thing that I think the children love the most is hugs and "I love you's" being given freely.

The part that I love the most is the altar ministry. Often, the children seek God for what they want from him. It usually goes something like this, "I just want my daddy or mommy to come home", and sometimes they pray, "I want them to just love me."

Today our youth ministry is full of these children who have grown to become youth. Some are still asking the same questions, still believing for their parents. Most are still holding on to the Father's hand. In just a few years they will be counted in the 80% of adults who met God before they turned 18 yrs. old.

The youth who started out with us have faced many hardships of this "current of destruction" that our church is surrounded by. The world is not kind to teenagers who are trying to live right. When they are successful they are beautiful and something to behold. Some of our most wonderful success stories are about these young saints. They love to be loved and smile and run to you to receive what you have. The are wonderful fruit, worth every cost and effort.

CHAPTER 13

Life Recovery Ministry

DANNY HARP came to our church one Sunday morning. I was delighted to see him. We talked after church and caught up on old times, not getting around to any important subject like, are you looking for a church and what's going on with your relationship with your other church. We said good-bye and he did not come back for a few services. I guess that I remember this because our church had been at about 85 people on average in attendance, then as if someone sounded a bell it went down to 9. So when one good man, a known disciple comes to visit, you remember.

What I learned later was that Danny had felt that God was leading him in a different direction and he felt that God had said to go to The Father's House. He told his pastor what he was thinking and did not get a favorable response. He told the pastor that he wanted his blessing and he would wait for it. In the meantime he went to his first pastor, who as you can imagine, he was still friends with because he is obviously a submitted man. Danny asked him what he should do. He said pray and wait on the Lord. Well his current pastor came around and gave his blessing, and Danny joined us in our work at The Father's House. At first he just played music with me and helped with the worship.

At the time Danny was working at a drug and alcohol recovery center, because he was a credentialed counselor. One day we were talking, I asked if he would like to join our staff, to counsel people suffering with addiction? He told me about his desire to have men live in his house, in a clean and sober environment.

I was building a house at our campus and told him that this could be our first house. I don't know what he thought about that, he did not have any idea how big my dream was. I am sure that as I told him what I believed the future held for us, he began to see a much larger vision as well. Out of these conversations and much prayer, Life Recovery Ministry, or LRM as we call it, was birthed.

First there was one home, then two and so on. In the beginning we actually were very easily conned by the clients and had a lot of failure, we thought that it was our inexperience and we had many lessons to learn.

Andy Engler came to Oroville on an outreach team from the Toronto School of Ministry and decided to return as an intern. He joined LRM as a house leader and we grew. Which resulted in more hurting people, lots of hard work. It took money, time, energy; all the same investments as any good ministry. The harvest was ripe and ready and the workers were in place and willing to bear the cost and gather the harvest. We pressed on with the belief that when the harvest is loved, the harvest becomes fruit, fruit that remains.

There is Katie who came to us from jail, she had been in Southside for several years and I had noticed her often. One day I saw her at a particular house where the inhabitants were involved in everything bad. She caught my attention and I remember praying. "Lord that girl is somebody's baby girl." At least that's how she started out, I wondered if she ever got a chance or was just let go to the wolves. I asked the Lord why do I get this blessed life, and she does not, why can't she have it?

I have these times of feeling this compassion about individuals often. After praying for Katie, I drove on. Then, one day I drove up and saw her at our ladies LRM house. I went straight to her so I could ask her why she was at our house. I found out that she was in the program, she had just arrived from jail. In the first days and even months she was rebellious to say the least, also we were beginning to learn her story.

She had been on her own since 13 years old, hanging out with the wrong crowd. I wonder if there is any other kind of crowd for a 13 year old on her own. She was on her own because she had run away from her mother and found out they don't return runaways to their homes any more. She was with a guy and got pregnant at 15. Her first baby was born at 16, her second at 19, her third at 21, all boys.

Seven months pregnant with her third son, she was beaten severely with a bottle by her boyfiend. She believed during this beating that she was going to die. She thought she was being punished for using drugs during her pregnancy. Because of being beaten, she was taken to the hospital where her blood was tested, Katie tested positive for drugs, they tested the baby, he tested clear but the trouble began. She began to use methamphedamines and was being drug tested regularly. One day she gave a dirty test and Child Protection Services was coming to take her children. Quickly, she took all of her kids to her mother. By doing this she was able to keep them from the foster care system and from being separated. Then Katie fell deeper into drugs which is when she began the use of needles. To support this habit, she began to make and sell meth.

The downward spiral continued as she went into more abusive relationships. She robbed a car wash and got arrested. Katie pleaded guilty and went to Valley State Prison for women and began to call on Jesus. She asked Jesus to help her get to a place where she could have clean friends and get help. They released her back in Oroville and one day she got drunk and was walking by the house of a Drug Court employee who called in to report her. Facing violation and more prison she accepted the placement at LRM.

She was stubborn, difficult, and rebellious. I do not believe that you can help people who do not want help and I was questioning if she wanted help. One day her house leader Rebecca asked us for a break from Katie, as she broke down and cried. Katie heard about it and began to think this is about me. She said, "I am a pain in her rear, Rebecca has loved me and all I have given her is grief." With this realization came the knowledge that she was just repeating the same pattern of rebellion and stubbornness that caused her to lose her children. Also, it was the same pattern that landed her in prison. She then began to submit, Katie began buying in, and she was listening.

John Arnott came to The Father's House one night and gave a call for ministry. Russell Smith was with him, praying for people and when he prayed for Katie she fell down and she stayed down. Katie Bruhn was changed, born again, baptized, flooded, immersed, filled with the Holy Spirit and changed. Katie had a one step program to finding God. She began to be happy. Katie had many more trials and tests but she was no longer alone. One of her biggest hurdles was losing her past identity.

This is going well, Katie became an intern at The Father's House Church and a house leader for LRM. After that she moved in with her mom to be mothering her children on more that just weekends. Katie is a world changer and born again believer. She even has a new name and she sits in the front row at church services with her new husband Dave Rodriquez. She will change many and be used mightily, she is a light in a dark world.

Dave Rodriquez was working on a foundation in a neighborhood that my company was also working in. I noticed him and began to pray each day that he could know God. It was no coincidence that he asked me for a job one day. God had set him up, Dave would hear of His love. It became very evident that he was not living right. Dave was trapped in a drug cycle, he became unreliable and I had to fire him.

I did not forget how God had put him on my heart. God had not forgot either. Dave came back and asked for a job and we tried again. When I shared the fact with him that God was after him, Dave would say, "I don't know why that is so hard for me, I would love to get my life right." People say this often, sometimes it is just wishful thinking and sometimes they truly want the madness to go away.

One day the time had arrived. I told Dave that it only took a twenty second prayer right here on this job site to find out if God was real. Did He reject you, was it too late for you, and the big what if, would He forgive you? Dave took the challenge and prayed with me right on that job site. You probably guessed it, GOD SHOWED UP.

Dave was touched by God and believed that his life would be different. But, there were other people involved, people in his life. His transformation into a disciple, and then a son, had one more relapse and trip through the county jail, where he prayed and studied the Bible.

When he got out of jail, he came right to The Father's House. It did not hurt that he had an ankle bracelet on and the only place that his house arrest would let him go was work and church. Anytime he wanted to get out of the house he had to go to church. He began to play the drums for our band and dedicated his gifts and talents to the Lord.

Dave became a house leader in LRM and even to this day people talk about his investment in their lives as their leader. He once told me that he wanted to get married and be a father but he was not physically able to have children. I said, "tell the Father."

Today he is married to Katie and sits in the front row at church services. When I looked down the isle at their wedding and saw him escorting their youngest son up to the front row, the two of them holding hands as father and son, I cried, before the wedding even started. The other two boys were in the wedding party and it was clear he had already become a father and was about to become a husband. Dave is a world changer, a disciple of Jesus, a son to his dad, who was the best man at his wedding. He is a good man, a man among men. Dave has every reason to hold his head up and look forward to hearing the words, *"well done my good and faithful servant."* I am proud of Dave and Katie, they truly are the best of the best and better than the rest, the fruit that remains. You will meet them in heaven and their children's children will rise up and call them blessed.

It is so good to sit back and think about the people who have crossed over from death to life. You could say that they had their life recovered. When you look at the circumstances that brought them to us, it is nothing short of miraculous.

CHAPTER 14

Lives Recovered

NICOLE, OUR daughter, was shopping for furniture one day when she began to talk to the salesman about the furniture that was being thrown out when people buy new. She asked if it could it be given to the intern program or to LRM. The salesman wanted to know more about the program so she told him. He began to understand that we are a discipleship program for drug and alcohol addiction and other life recovery issues. He then told Nicole about his daughter who was deep in the drug lifestyle and who had recently had asked him for help getting out. After talking with Nicole he began following the leads to begin the process of getting his daughter into LRM.

She interviewed with our team and they told her that since she needed financial considerations she would have to return to church the following evening to talk with Pastor Steve. I interviewed her and thought that she was only half-way ready. She wanted to be free but wanted parts of her old life as well. Also I did not believe that she liked being told what to do, so I highlighted the part about the fact that we are going to tell you what to do. When you can sleep, eat, or where you can go. For the first thirty days we will ground you with no outside contact or visits. We call this thirty day beginning blackout.

Her name is Kylee and I would have given her a week before she "blew this popcorn stand." If the guy that she was hooked up with, her partner in crime, had not been in a program at the time and out of touch, Kylee probably would not have stayed. She had been out there since thirteen years old when her life had been consumed by competitive swimming and her daddy was her hero. First, her swim coach got fired from his position and her dad who had been charged with fraud was taken to serve a term in prison. Her mother seemed lost without her husband and Kylee was left to herself.

She began with pot but graduated to oxicodone very soon. As she scrounged for money every day to get her drugs, she found herself dopesick and desperate one day. She was able to get a couple of pills and went with a friend to use them. The friend made them into liquid and put them in a needle so Kylee was stuck, sick, and in need. She began the life of shooting dope with needles. Kylee very soon found out that you could sell the oxicodone for money and buy a lot more heroin, which she began to do. At fifteen years old shooting heroin running amuck, partying.

The days turned into months, then years, living this "I don't care lifestyle," until she got arrested. She was working all the angles and when faced with jail time she would go to rehab. Twenty eight days in rehab and this cute little girl telling the judge that she was a victim. Also telling him that she "desperately wants help." That's her ticket to freedom from the system.

Often times parents help their children with the process of conning the judge. It's hard to believe that your child should go to prison or is just straight up lying to your face. Most parents in the early phase of their child's drug addiction are finding out that their baby cannot be trusted. Usually, it is a very expensive lesson. Kylee's parent's lessons were no exception. They finally reached the point of being fed up, they had been ripped off and lied to. Unless she went to another rehab, they were going to press charges for all of the things that she had done to them. After this very expensive twenty eight day rehab, Kylee went to clean and sober living where she met a man, and her "I don't care" attitude quickly returned and they were off and running, down to San Diego.

These two went over the border to Mexico to buy drugs on a daily basis, walking across with a carefree attitude that did not draw attention. Then they would sell some of the drugs and use some, in a vicious cycle of bondage, but feeling like they were completely free, and the smartest people in the world. Until one day when Kylee went alone to buy the drug supply and the inevitable happened. This young lady was alone in Mexico with a drug dealer who forced himself upon her. I believe that her self confidence began to crumble and this world of drugs did not look so good anymore. She was an addict and needed the drugs that they were getting in Mexico. Even being raped was not enough incentive to run to help. They moved up to Santa Rosa and continued to deal drugs and buy from the same source only from a little farther away.

The young man she was with left her alone and went to rehab. Kylee was left dealing on her own. One couple that she had gotten hooked on drugs and was supplying drugs to, asked to know who her drug supplier was. She introduced them to her supplier, which was an unfortunate mistake. They did not need her any more, she could not make money selling them drugs. She was hurting for drugs, had no place to go, no man to protect her in this drug world and she became very vulnerable. This couple had a plan for her, if she would prostitute herself for them and live with them as a threesome, they would give her a place to live and take care of all her drug needs as well.

At first she agreed, that night they used drugs all night. In the morning realizing what she had agreed to and what the future held for her, she prayed a desperate prayer to God, "I will do anything if you free me from addiction." She checked into a hospital to detox, and called her dad to say that she was ready.

This is where Nicole, my daughter walked into a furniture store and talked to her dad. After the interviews and the process of Kylee getting into the program, she still did not have a plan to stay. As soon as this guy gets out of rehab she is going to join him and they will live happily ever after together.

About a month or two into her program, at a Wednesday night church service, during worship, she was sitting there. Her house leader Rebecca, came up behind her to pray for her. A wave of God's love surrounded her, she knew that God loved her and she was "born again."

Kylee completed her stay in LRM and did fantastic. She applied to our intern program and is one of the best of the best. We asked her to be a house leader and she is giving her life away for the blessing of others. Kylee is in her second year of internship as a small group leader. Which is her third year with The Father's House. She is definitely the fruit that remains and she is producing fruit in others, using her unique experiences to minister to people who are struggling with the life of addiction.

I am unable to imagine a more rewarding ministry experience than when the fruit of our lives is people who were in miserable situations now living life abundantly, taking what they have received and giving it away for the benefit of others.

CHAPTER 15

The Fruit of the Spirit

THE FRUIT of the Spirit is the most important fruit in any endeavor that claims to be of God. The deception that goes on in God's name, whether that is in Christianity, a cult or Judaism or any other group that claims a great father creator is most easily seen in their fruit.

All men feel the presence of God. All men feel the right and wrong of things, at some time in their lives. If I want to know if someone is of God, or what they are saying is right then I should look at their results, I must look at their fruit. What should their fruit be, if they are God's servant? What do you look for? Well the first thing that I look for is what do they live for? What is their life about? Is it selfless or selfish?

The second thing that I look for is what is the outcome of these values? Do they live what they believe? And is there harvest in it? Some people I know have many children, raising disciples to the Lord. The outcome of their life and the conclusion of whether they have done it

God's way is seen in the character of their children. Raising children is a lifetime commitment. If I am going to read someone's book or follow someone's example on how to raise children, I am going to look at their children and see if their methods work. Is there evidence that what they have done produces the fruit of the Spirit.

The fruit of the Spirit; peace, patience, kindness, love, and the rest, these are the fruit that we need to learn how to value. We should ask ourselves, are these the results that we see coming from the things that we value? It really should be love, joy, peace, patience, kindness and self control and *"the greatest of these is love"* as the measuring rod in our lives. Is there love in our fruit basket, and is there love in the fruit basket of the people and religions that we follow? Giving your life away and being selfless, loving others more than you love yourself, peace, joy and the rest is the fruit of the Spirit.

Love all by itself is probably the most misunderstood and ignored of the fruit. Of all the sayings of Jesus there is much missed about the one thing that Jesus was trying to get us to do as Christians, *"love one another as I have loved you."* We spend much time, sermon space and lots of Christian discussion about all the things we are not supposed to do like sexual stuff and drinking and immoral behavior. Yet the most important thing that Jesus wanted us to do was believe in the one the Father sent us and then love one another as he loved us.

A lot is said about loving God with all of our heart, mind, soul and strength. Yet Jesus was telling a Jewish man how to fulfill the Law when He said that. Jesus told His disciples that if they wanted to know how to recognize who loved Him, they should look for him who obeys Jesus' commands. The only command that Jesus ever gave was to *"love one another as I have loved you."* What about loving one another as Jesus loved us? To love others is to love Him, John said. To do for others and meet their needs is to love them.

The good Samaritan was the neighbor who loved because he saw the need of the man in the ditch and served him. No need to discuss any further, the fruit tells the story of who the Samaritan is. Does he love? Don't ask him, just look at him.

If we want revival to be part of movements and churches, then we ought to look for the fruit of the Spirit. The Spirit must be evident or manifested by its fruit. For instance, in times of great turmoil it is particularly difficult to maintain peace. Peace that passes understanding would be fruit that the Spirit is present. Sometimes we are trying to do a Jesus ministry and yet it does not seem like God will finance it, sometimes even when we have been really generous it feels like you actually can out give God. We even get mad at Him. Then He reminds us that without faith it is impossible to please God. Peace in good times is easy. Peace in turmoil is spelled FAITH or TRUST and with these growing all over your branches, money trouble does not seem as overwhelming. The evidence that someone knows God is in their fruit, the outcome and results of that relationship. Jesus said, "*you will know the tree by its fruit.*"

How does one know that they themselves are living in faith? I think that we look at our lives and see if the fruit of love is there. That is why Paul said in the Word that "faith, hope, and love remains but the greatest of these is love". If self examination determines that I do have the fruit of loving others as I have been loved, I would say that the other fruit can be had as well.

We should be asking ourselves if we think that we are doing right or wrong. We should ask, if people follow me will they get closer to God or not? Will they get lost or not? What is the outcome and results of my Christianity? If the answer to these questions do not have the right answers then I should change how I live my faith, how I operate my Christianity.

CHAPTER 16

Being Christian

BEING CHRISTIAN is something I think about often. I am Christian, The Father's House Church is a Christian church, Steve Orsillo Construction is often referred to as a Christian business. The word Christian means little Christ. Also, the Christ is the anointed one. So, being Christian is being the little anointed one. I am to be a replica of Christ, a little anointed one. A business must reflect the character of Christ to be a Christian business, a church must be doing the work of Christ and teaching the principles of Christ to be a Christian church. Jesus said, *"why do you call me Lord and yet do not do the things that I teach you to do."* If having Jesus as Lord is defined as being a replica of him, then doing what He says would be the action or fruit of being Christian.

People have given me many titles in my life, some have called me boss, pastor, brother, father, yet the one I love the most is 'Christian'. I AM CHRISTIAN. I want my life to reflect the Christ who is Jesus the Lord. If He is my Lord, it would be seen in the fact that I do what He says.

Jesus took some disciples up on a mountain, where He was visited by Elijah and Moses. These disciples saw them, and said *"let us build an altar for each of you."* They wanted to worship them equally. A cloud then formed and a voice spoke out of the mist, *"THIS IS MY SON, LISTEN TO HIM."* This voice is very obviously the Father's voice, He says clearly *"LISTEN TO JESUS."* Here we have the law giver in Moses, the great prophet in Elijah, both standing there with Jesus and the Father tells the Apostles, who will carry the message of what being Christian is, *"LISTEN TO JESUS."* One of them, Peter, who would at a later time have to answer the questions about mixing the law and the gospel for non-Jewish Christians, would I believe remember this day and set for us the standard and say, *"Now therefore why do you put God to the test by placing upon the neck of the disciples a yoke which neither our fathers nor we have been able to bear?"* It was as if Peter was reminded of this day on the mountain and remembered that the Father wanted them to concentrate their listening and their living of this faith in Jesus. It seems like the Father did not want three altars built of stone but one built on obedience to the words of Jesus.

I think today as I listen to Christian speakers on media outlets, I get a sense that they would rather teach from the law and the prophets and make them equals just as these great apostles wanted to do. The Father today wants to remind us that nothing has changed, He is still saying, *"LISTEN TO JESUS."*

Jesus is saying now, just what He said then. Things like He said in John chapter 12, *"He who believes in me, believes not in me but Him who sent me. And he who sees me sees Him who sent me. I have come as a light into the world, that whosoever believes in me should not remain in darkness, and if anyone hears my words and does not believe, I do not judge him; for I did not come to judge the world but to save the world. He who rejects me, and does not receive my words, has that which judges him-the word that I have spoken will judge him in the last day. For I have not spoken on my own authority; but the Father who sent me gave me a command, what I should say and what I should speak.*"

It is clear that Jesus considers His words to be the will of the Father. He says His words will be the judge of us. Not in what He says but in what we do with His words. Our deeds will determine if we reject him, or if we receive him. They will decide if we love Him, "He who has my commandments and keeps them, it is he who loves me."

They, the words of Jesus, *they* will judge us. How we respond to His words will tell whether we love Him, and they will reveal the truth of the statement that He is our Lord. This will be determined by our doing what He said. Is this what the Father meant when He told the apostles to *"LISTEN TO JESUS?"*

Even what makes us to be considered a sheep or a goat will be determined by what we do with the words of Jesus to love our neighbors. In Matthew chapter 25, He finishes the story of the sheep and goats by saying, *"whatsoever you did not do for the least of these, you did not do for me. Then they will go away to eternal punishment, but the righteous (the doers) to eternal life."* That's how he finishes this story. Now, if you major on anything but that He wants us to do something to help the hungry, the thirsty and the imprisoned, I believe that you would not be *"listening"* to the words of Jesus, which are the instructions of the Father on the mount of transfiguration.

So, to be known as a Christian, I believe, would be defined by the fact that a person lives according to the words of Jesus, or you could say, he does the words of Jesus.

I recently began to pay attention to how many messages that I listened to were preached from the words of Jesus. I listened at conferences and to the radio, then television. I found that on most days eight out of ten of the messages that I heard never spoke of the words of Jesus. He was mentioned in most of them as praised and glorified, but His teachings and instructions were not the focus of the majority of the teachings.

If I am going to be punished eternally, or judged by, or found to be following the Father's instructions, based on my doing of the instructions of Jesus, wouldn't it be important that I major on the teachings of Jesus? It seems that we have it backwards. The majority of what we are hearing is not the teachings of Jesus. We are not hearing what the Father of Heaven and the Lord over all the earth said that we should listen to, the very words which Jesus said would judge us, the very thing which would determine our eternal life or punishment. It seems that we need to have a season of hearing the words of Jesus and being strongly encouraged to do them.

I began to look at the requests that I received for help from various ministries. I started asking, are they doing Jesus things? Are they Jesus ministries?

Occasionally, I am invited to prayer events; most of these events don't really follow the Jesus model. Jesus wanted us to pray, so, I joined Jesus in the school of prayer, letting Jesus be the teacher. Isn't that what the Father said, *"listen to Jesus"*? Jesus said, *"when you pray, don't pray in vain repetition but instead pray, our Father in heaven hallowed be thy name."* Jesus continues in His instructions and prohibits praying to be seen. If I am going to err, I would like to err on the side of trying to accomplish what He says. Are the things that we are spending our lives on the things that make us look like Jesus? Do they make me resemble Him? Are they about loving the, *"least of these my brethren,"* or being a neighbor?

At The Father's House, we have been following a course that the Lord gave me 30 years ago. On Sunday mornings we study the Gospels and in the midweek services we study the teachings of the apostles, the men who heard His words and went out to live them. Men like Paul who was recommended to us by Peter the apostle. We have never, and unless God gives us a new assignment, we will never change.

Come in ten years and you will find the same, a verse by verse, every sentence read, study on the words and teachings of Jesus. A friend of mine asked me, "what about all the stuff that is not powerful or interesting?" I said, that I had never found any verse that God could not teach us important things from.

It is great to never worry about what you are preaching next. Jesus is the perfect theology and if you have seen him you have seen the Father. You want a perfect revelation of the Father? See Jesus, study Him and meditate on His words day and night. Make Him your first thought in the morning and your last thought at night. Inspect yourself on only one subject, ask yourself only one question, do I look like Jesus in the world? Then you know, you qualify as being Christian.

CHAPTER 17

In My Name

A VERY important promise that Jesus made about being Christian is that we could pray in the name of Jesus. Now I have believed at times that saying the name of Jesus is the same as praying in the name of Jesus. Like saying the name makes the difference, as if prayer that is said to be in the name of Jesus makes the prayer more valuable no matter what the actions or character of the person praying is. Just say "in the name of Jesus," and everything should happen just as you say it.

When Jesus was asked by the disciples *"Lord teach us to pray,"* He answered, *"when you pray do not pray in vain repetitions like the gentiles do, but when you pray say this; our Father who is in heaven, hallowed be your name."*

This instruction to *"hallow"* His name is probably not the same as using or saying His name. I believe it means something along the line of, I honor your name and I will not dishonor it. It could also be the same as saying, I am in the name of your son and call you My Father. Prayer to "Our Father" means that I am a son and I would expect the request to be answered. If I am praying and I believe that I am in the name of Jesus, I actually resemble Him, then I receive what Jesus would receive.

For most of man's history, fathers have wanted their sons to carry out their affairs with the understanding that what they do and how they conduct their business affects the honor of their name. What a father does reflects on the sons. What a son does is attributed to how he was raised or the stature of his father. Honoring the name of the father is not a new idea and only seems to have confused the children of our time. No one would wonder what it meant to say that the sins of the father are visited on the sons for several generations, in any time before say 1920. To hallow your father's name was to honor it, to value it, to know that you will not dishonor the name that you hallow. To do this one must have an investment in the name. One must believe that the name his father gave him was valuable.

I think of my youngest son Anthony, he is talented beyond my imagination. He is so comfortable in front of a crowd and has really good things to say, but he has very little experience. When Anthony gets up in front of people I am reminded that being an Orsillo he reflects on me. He was asked to preach or share for the first time at a 'true love waits' gathering in our city.

People from every church were there with their teenagers to support the message that waiting to have sex until marriage was the definition of true love. Well Anthony had zero experience with sex, or multi denominational gatherings. I must say, his lack of experience and his lack of fear as a combination had me fidgeting in my chair, yet I did not interfere. I know some of you have an Anthony in your life and you understand these kind of gatherings, you know what I mean.

Anthony began, it was awesome! From the start to finish he nailed it, good words, huge anointing, very well delivered. I wanted to stand up and shout, that's my son, his name is Orsillo. Yep that's right, he is with me.

I began to share with pastor friends what he taught that night. One pastor who was the leader of a large congregation was about to start a series on the subject of sex. He asked if he could use the illustration that Anthony had used. He promised of course to give Anthony the credit, yep I said it's ANTHONY ORSILLO. He came in my name, as always he honored it, what was I worried about, it is his name also. Then it hit me, he looks like me, he lives by the principles I had taught him, he is a very obedient son, he calls me father and honors my name. If another human being could imitate Anthony and convince me that he was my son, I think that guy could ask me anything and if it were in my power, I would do it for him.

I guess that I am trying to make the connection that being a Christian should be an imitation of Jesus and that to come in the name means that we should look, sound, and act like the person, not just use his name. Which makes the words of Jesus, "*ask my Father anything in my name and He will do it for you,*" make more sense than just believing that saying His name is the same as, "in His name."

My daughter Nicole struggled with the idea that she would give up her name when she got married. We value our name, to give it up is an act of love for the person that you give it up for. It is just your name as long as you do not think about it. Then when you consider that it is honored as your father has given it honor, it becomes more difficult to let that go.

The seven sons of Sceva saw that Paul used a name that had a lot of power. Paul commanded demons in the name of Jesus. So these sons of Sceva thought, we will do the same and the spirits will obey us as well. The demons knew that when these sons of Sceva used a name that wasn't theirs and had no authority to use, that name had no power over them. In this story the demon got a little upset. Before giving the sons of Sceva a thrashing they delivered a most interesting and revealing message. The demon said, "*I recognize Jesus, and I know about Paul, but who are you?*" The power and authority is certainly not in borrowing the right name.

Do the demons know that you have the same last name as Jesus?

Do they know that you have a right to use His name? Do they know that you go by the name Christian? Do they know that you are coming in His name?

If one of my sons or daughters went to someone in my church and said my dad wants something to be done, the people in my church would know that they come in my name, this is his son or this is his daughter. This son or daughter probably has permission and authority to use his name.

Jesus said, *"By this all men will know that you are my disciples, that you love one another."* The one who lives this way probably has permission and authority to use Jesus' name.

CHAPTER 18

Father I Have Shown Forth Your Name to Them

IN CASE you may wonder if you know what "*coming in His name*" would look like, I recommend the words of Jesus as a starting point. He said, "*Father I have shown forth your name to them.*" He said this just before He was to leave them and He was praying for them. It seems that having shown forth the Father's name gave Jesus great comfort. He was leaving his sons and they would be all right because He had "*shown forth*" the Father's name to them. Now most commentators that I have read say that this phrase "*shown forth*" means that Jesus had demonstrated the Father's name, not just taught them His name.

Since the beginning God's name was very mysterious and the people of Israel were not even able to speak it, all very scary stuff. God was even called by some "The God who has no name." Moses asked Him what His name was and He said that the fact that He was The Present One was his name. Some people just want to call Him a familiar name, in our culture maybe it would be Bob. Bob the God, or God whose name is Bob. Wouldn't that be awful? Most people today just want His name to be God. Very generic, just God. No specific nature or characteristics implied. People from their day called their gods names that were associated with nature like Rah, the God of the Sun, Yet the answer to Moses' question was not a common name but a wonderful characteristic, "*I AM WITH YOU*," this truth about Him is what He wanted to be known by. All through the history of God's interaction with man He has mostly been know by His actions. Jesus says "*Father I have shown forth your name to them.*" "*Father,*" He called Him. Father reveals more about our God than any other word or name could.

The next step to knowing God's name would be to SEE JESUS, and look where He told us to look, which was at Him when He said, "*when you have seen me you've seen the Father,*" or "*I and the Father are one.*" This makes more sense when you consider these words together with "*I have manifested Your name to the men whom You gave Me out of the world.*" He said this in a prayer for them as a statement that He had done what it took to protect them, that they would be all right because they had seen His name.

I must conclude that the way Jesus showed them the Father's name was by showing it through His name and saying, "*ask anything, do anything, pray anything or believe anything in my name.*" Then the very first effort of the Christian who is going to live his life in the center of God's will would be to LISTEN TO JESUS, and SEE JESUS, then IMITATE JESUS and see how His name has been shown forth.

When I want to know what that looks like in me and what name Jesus showed forth to them I think about the things that God has been called like "*The Bright Morning Star*" and I can really see Him in that. My personal favorite is "*Father*" because it really reveals something about me and my relationship with Him. It also shows His intentions towards me. Then there is the whole list of Jehovah names like *"Jirah"* or *"The Provider,"* I get great comfort in that, it brings about peace. There are so many more characteristics of God's name in what Jesus has *"shown forth"* like *"Savior"* and *"healer"* plus *"teacher,"* not to forget *"bread of life"*, *"the living water."* No comment is necessary is it, just read the name and it brings comfort and accomplishes what Jesus wanted it to. It reveals and continues to reveal that the Father's love is in us.

How about this one, *"IMMANUEL"* God is with us.

Or *"Author and finisher of our faith."*

"The rock of our salvation," it gives me goose bumps.

Can you handle more? *"The lover of my soul."*

How about *"soon coming King"* which brings to mind *"The Alpha and Omega."*

"The Creator of all things," and *"The Word of God."*

Or my all time favorite *"The lamb of God who takes away the sins of the world,"* (my world.)

In so many places He called Him *"your Father"* or *"my Father."* Do we now have a Father in Heaven? Talk about highly placed family. Is this what He meant by *"I have shown forth your name to them."* If Jesus has *"shown forth"* the Father's name to us and revealed who He is to us, then I really like what I have seen so far and really want to live in the purpose that God has shown me. One that the apostle John shared with us in his gospel, *"that the love you have for me, would be in them and that I would be in them."*

I want to be the house of the Father's love and the home of Jesus. I also want these names to 'show forth in me'. People who look at me should see the nature of God. They should be able to see that the *"Prince of Peace"* is in me. I can learn a great deal and receive revelation about God from His names, what He will and will not do and who He is. Others that seek him will find him by watching me. I want to *"show forth his name to them."*

CHAPTER 19

Wine in a World Full of Water

I HAVE often wondered about Jesus' coming out miracle, turning water into wine. It is obvious that this unveiling of God in the flesh had been planned for many centuries of man. It was not by His mother's whim that he found Himself being coerced into coming out as the miracle doing Messiah, announcing that the Deliverer is here. I mean arriving in a stable and being revealed to poor shepherds is beautiful, especially to someone who was born poor and of no privilege. Riding a donkey makes sense if you want to arrive in occupied Jerusalem and be seen and known by the people yet not threaten the occupying governor or cause the people to start a revolution. I believe that everything Jesus did had a purpose, so this water into wine miracle must be part of the plan.

I love the study of Jesus. Andrew Murray wrote a book called With

Christ In The School of Prayer. I love this title. I want my life to be With Christ in The School of everything. The idea being that in whatever I do, I should want Jesus to be my teacher and example. So, what is He teaching us in Cana of Galilee? Well I did not have to look very deep to see this, He turned water into wine. What is this water that Jesus would change it? Why does He change it, He is God? Does Jesus need to use water? Why can't He make wine out of air? I thought on these questions and came to these conclusions. Water is very important to man's survival, and unlike air one must work to get water, especially in Jesus' time. It has value and having done so much work to get it, would you trade it for wine? Probably if you were desperate for wine. Water is also very common, everyone has water, and at this wedding they had lots of water. What they needed was wine. The time had come where a demonstration of the anointed one's purpose on earth was in order.

He was going to take something very common and ordinary, and cause it to become born again as wine. Not just any wine, but as the story goes, *"the best wine."* It dawns on me that we are still talking about this wine two thousand years later. This is some wine! It stands out, first to the steward, then to the apostle, then to Christians for all of time. The Lord must want to come out and reveal Himself to us in a very special way. I believe that Jesus wants the world to begin to know that He has come to change things. Jesus has come to do things and change things, the things that He came to change are not about water or wine. If you see that Jesus can change water and wine, you will begin to believe that He can change you! He wants you to change from something common and everyday to something the experts and tasters will say is the best.

The message of Jesus has not always been received that way in history but I believe it is Jesus' intention that His message be demonstrated that way. We can be made brand new. We can be new wine in a world full of water. If there is no new wine, Jesus will take the ordinary water that is just sitting around and make it *"born again"* into something beautiful. You and I were probably somewhat common when Jesus found us and He is coming out in our lives, to show us that He can do a miracle in our lives to make us brand new. He will make us "*the best.*"

I stand at the front of the church and watch people coming in to our services. I think they are coming here mostly because they want to be something different than what they are. The different thing that they want to be, they have dreamed was something special or even beautiful. They hope and trust that something will happen to them because they came to church. Maybe some believe my words will change them, you know, make their lives all different. Many have already been born again and they just want to be used by the Lord, filled by Him, express their hearts to Him and hear the word of God. The others, the seekers, they come in all different states of mind. The ones that I feel sorry for are the ones who do not seek Him, but they seek His church, or the man of God, the atmosphere. Sometimes it is just the comfort that comes from tradition that they seek. They don't all come to receive the miracle of Jesus changing them and their lives.

I think the best lesson in Cana was that the miracle happened because Jesus' mother knew who He was, God become man, and she sought the power therein. She pleaded with Jesus to help them by doing this miracle. Then others would begin to know who He was.

I tell the people that He is seeking to reach them. That Jesus is what they need to be "*born again.*" Religion has done such a great job of promoting itself, people just cannot see past religion even if you're shouting the truth and demonstrating the fruit. They often leave the same as they came, not becoming the new wine, not becoming Christlike. The church is not a wine skin to them; it's just a water barrel. They do not go away feeling the comforting, guiding, counseling or fruit bearing power that most of us wish they could receive. Water barrels are good and people need them, there are plenty of water barrels around though. What I want The Father's House to be is a wineskin, full of people who have been changed, "*born again*" into new wine. I want people who want to be new wine, and who want to lead others to be **wine in a water filled world**, born again by the ministry and love of Jesus.

Jesus is the revelation of the Father; He is the Father's voice and His will. Do you want to know God, the King of heaven and Lord over all the earth? Look at Jesus, imitate him and submit to His ministry. Are you tired of being like everyone around you, common, ordinary? Are you tired of being a church or ministry, even a Christian who just does what everyone else says is right? Then study Jesus, He is the perfect doctrine. The perfect church by-laws and mission statement would read simply, "*SEE JESUS.*"

I wish that people had never had a different first impression of Jesus than that He wants to make something different of them, something special like He did with the wine. If they had not had a different first impression, I think they would also wish be a spectacle, changed into something special like **wine in a water filled world.**

The perfect book series would probably be, With Jesus in the School of Loving People, and With Jesus in the School of Giving, or the next School book with Jesus as the teacher, Praying, Trusting, or How Should We Then Live. What a series that would make, a study in the life and times and teachings of Jesus the Christ of God. I love the Old Testament, in it God shows me who He is and what life would be like without grace. All of the questions are in this old covenant. The description of the Christ is in there, how else would I recognize Him? I have found the answer. I do not need to re-study the question. I am a Jesus man, I was called a Jesus freak when I was young. I said "thank you, that is the nicest thing that anyone has ever called me." Once someone said that I was, "too heavenly minded to be any earthly good." The idea just excited me more, can you imagine what would happen if heaven and earth were actually to dwell together commonly in me? Like what, "too heavenly minded to be any earthly good" actually means. So heavenly minded that I was no good to the world's system. A man who could accomplish that would disrupt the world so much, why the world would have to crucify him. So many questions are raised by this revelation that Jesus wants to change you into something really special. If you're wondering about the answer to almost any question, "SEE JESUS," He has the answer. Sadly enough, people criticized me for what I believed. I was a young Christian and I got sidetracked for a season. Now, I am back on the trail of having me and my church and anyone else who will listen, pursue the *"let Your kingdom come, let Your will be done, here just as it is in Heaven."* I am the Father's son, I carry the Father's name, I will not dishonor it. Father cause me to reflect this message. To accept that Jesus said it and to not listen to anyone but Jesus. The title of the book on our lives would be, With Jesus in the School of How We Should Then Live.

CHAPTER 20

The City that God Gave Us

WE WERE just living as Christians when God sent us to Oroville, California. It is a city with a very poor reputation. Recently a couple from Edmonton, Alberta were moving to Oroville to join us. They had come through Toronto School of Ministry and when they told people from that church where they were going, people were excited for them. They also went through the school of ministry at Bethel Church in Redding, California, which is near the town of Oroville. When they told friends there where they were going these people responded saying "I'm sorry" or "why"?

While I was going through the church adoption process I was in a church in Chico, California. As I was there with my family, the guy doing the announcements was doing his humorous routine by telling Oroville jokes. Anytime we tell anyone in Northern California that we are from Oroville, they almost cannot help but have facial expressions that are less than wonderful. When my wife and I were trying to figure out where God was sending us I had said that Oroville was the last place that I wanted to go, so I certainly understand their feelings on the subject.

Oroville was a large part of the Gold rush of the late 1800's. The Gold rush established a spirit of greed that is unbelievably still present today. The pilfering of Oroville's natural resources and the fact that her natural wealth is so often taken elsewhere results in the people of Oroville very seldom receiving the benefits that should accompany these resources.

I was led as I mentioned before to prayer walk and fast to find out the root of these results, that seem to hang like a cloud over this incredibly beautiful city. You see, Oroville's foothills are some of the most gorgeous hills that you could find, including a lake that is rich in beauty and wildlife is named Lake Oroville, The Feather River meanders right through downtown and is one of the most peaceful and wonderful sights I have ever seen. The people are friendly and warm. And yet it is clear that this city has a problem that it has not overcome. I thought that somebody ought to ask God what that problem was, so I did.

One night we got together as a church and formed a circle, there were about twenty five of us and we formed a circle facing out. It was the city that I wanted to find out about, so we faced the city in all directions. We said, "Lord tell us, what is the prince of the power of the air of this city that has held it hostage for so many years"? It did not take long to get an answer, you see He wants the city to be free more that I do. There I was holding pen in hand, notepad at the ready waiting to start writing the answer. When the Lord said, "selfishness" I wrote it down, then I said "Lord, I want to know the demonic prince of the power of the air, could you tell us his name". He said, "selfishness". I told him that I did not understand, could He tell me again if that really was the name of the demonic force that held the city of Oroville hostage for so many years. He said, "selfishness". The night ended with that being the only word that anyone received. Which in itself was unique.

The next day I went to a pastor's prayer meeting, it is a small gathering of pastors mostly around the neighborhood that we call Southside. I asked them what they thought was the answer to the question, what is the name of the prince of the power of the air that holds Oroville back? They had many answers, not one of which was selfishness.

One asked why I had asked, I told them my story. He began to rip through his Bible to the Book of Numbers while he said that God had shown him something that morning that he did not understand.

It was the story of where the Lord showed Moses the promised land and then said to him, because of your whoredom you will not go in, but you will wander around the desert until all have died and your sons will inherit this promise. Whoredom was then described as when a man does what is right in his own eyes or is right for himself instead of the whole crowd. Whoredom is selfishness.

Many had come to Oroville with the promise that God wanted to change the outcome. They had struggled with the spirit that held Oroville hostage for a time, usually giving up, which I can understand and do not blame them for. Then the city would miss out on the freedom from this whoredom that is firmly embedded in her from top to bottom and then when God sent the next Christians to start a stand against this spirit they receive resistance in the name of-been-there-done-that-and-I-own-the-t-shirt. They would meet complete apathy and indignation that someone would even try. Now I am not putting the people of Oroville down, this is a spirit.

I asked business people that would come to Oroville from other places what they thought about doing business in our city. They would say that people didn't trust each other, they worried that they would not get their share or that someone was taking advantage of them. These business people sometimes would just give up.

For me, God had shown me a promise of a great salvation revival and a time where everyone who sought the Lord would find what they sought Him for. He wanted to give the world a message from the city of Oroville. Oroville is a promised land and the prince of the power of the air is selfishness. Every malady that afflicted Oroville was rooted in selfishness and there is a very powerful spirit here that has enslaved people and even fed their desire to do what was right for themselves regardless of the effects it had on others.

CHAPTER 21

The Opposite Spirit

WE BEGAN to ask the Lord, what do we do? "Operate in the opposite spirit" was the answer. The, "operate in the opposite spirit" season of The Father's House began. The opposite spirit of selfishness would be unselfishness. Random acts of unselfishness became the purpose of the church.

We started with the visions that God had given us to change a neighborhood. We began taking a dump truck around the neighborhood and knocking on doors asking people if we could help them clean their yard. We also swept glass out of the streets. We determined that anything we did in our youth and kids programs would be free, for as long as we could afford to do them.

Our children's camp outs were an eye opener and learning experience; the parents would drop off their kids and just drive away not even asking us who the heck we were. Some kids would not have sleeping bags or anything that they needed for a camp out. Their parents heard that they could place their kids with someone for the weekend and they just could not wait for the party to begin. We would be chasing them down the road yelling for them to stop. They almost always did but were usually mad at us for bothering them. We explained that we had to have contact information, medical release forms and parent permission slips signed or these kids would be left behind. This was very confusing and a huge dilemma because in some cases it was not their parent who dropped them off. Of course all of these conditions were spelled out in the information packet that was sent around with the children.

Our youth camps cost one hundred sixty dollars per kid and we had busted a gut getting them all paid for. This is not a ministry for the faint hearted, it is for only those who have counted the cost and are ready to pay, then they will see the incredible fruit that remains in their ministry. The "*those who are forgiven much, love much*", kind of results.

We try to be at most city wide events like the light parade at Christmas time or the Feather Fiesta days where we try to give out something that says that we love Oroville. We have given out as many as twenty five hundred cups of hot chocolate at one parade, candy canes at another.

If we have a motto it is, "give your life away". People that have caught the bug have picked up 300,000 pounds of garbage from the streets and alley ways. They have worked with the authorities to get hundreds of abandoned cars removed from the streets of Southside.

We have these yard sales where everything is free, tons of wonderful clothes and household items. Also; Fall Festivals and neighborhood barbecues, all free food and lots of family games and fun for the kids.

Our Christmas gift program is called Gift of Hope. This year we supplied gifts for six hundred children, all free to the families. So many businesses and ordinary people of Oroville contributed to this program, which spreads the "in the opposite spirit" around and begins breaking the spirit of whoredom on the city.

I wish it would be quick but the spirit took hold with the permission of the church in Oroville. It has had a hold on Oroville for over one hundred and fifty years. It might take a few years to get people in Oroville to accept operating in this opposite spirit.

When I first came to Oroville I noticed that the churches did not do a lot of service to the community. Oh, they did fund raisers and self promoting but not just giving to show God's love.

A friend of mine Michael Tomlinson, a pastor of an after care church, also a former heroin addict and former resident of San Quentin, California, did a great deal of this kind of service for people. He would always declare that he was your servant, as he would do and still will do anything for you. The "warriors" as he would call them would all come in these vans and go to work. Now I must say that Pastor Michael T as we call him, is my inspiration for the LRM ministry that we do. He was operating in the opposite spirit. But, in Oroville it was rare to see this kind of servant ministry.

Today if you read the religious section of the newspaper, you will see announcements of different churches doing services for people, compassion ministry, giveaways, outreaches in parks with free food. I believe there is a trend that is happening in our city. I am excited because I can see the reversal of selfishness.

Selflessness is the fruit of Christianity, or it is called love as defined by Jesus. Selflessness is the spirit that sets people free, it is the spirit that sets churches free. Selflessness is what you need the church to operate in to change a city. It is the power of the gospel, it is the loving of our neighbors. Selflessness is Jesus' ministry, or it is a ministry of Jesus. When selflessness rules our hearts, someone might say "Jesus is here."

The Mount Olives Food Bank is a garage that we store food in, a garage that we have had to air condition and stack with refrigerators and freezers, along with shelves floor to ceiling. From this garage with the fancy name we feed people every Monday. They line up at the campus and sometimes it is hours early, sometimes the line is long, real long! When you look at the food and then you look at the line, all you can do is pray. It is a miracle, everyone gets food. One couple who ran the food bank would go out and buy a truck load of stuff and fill the boxes. Sometimes it is LRM clients who have to do it, they empty all of the food from the residence houses on Mondays and I wait for the complaints, they don't come. Everyone gets a box.

Recently, we were very strapped for money because in the summer we had six hundred dollar power bills from the refrigerators and freezers. I had to begin the process of telling people that we might not be able to continue the food bank. Well this was bad news to some of the people in my church, they had been hungry as children, and as addicts they had to go without. This food bank is very important to them.

I told a friend of mine, his name is Dave, about the problem and he said that he and his father in-law wanted to help. One of the costs of the food bank was traveling to Sacramento each Thursday and getting a truckload of food from the Gleaners Food Bank. Dave's father-in-law Doug was part of a men's group and they attend the Oroville Church of the Nazarene. Doug committed to organizing these men to do this pick up each Thursday and deliver the food to our food bank.

I could not have planned this better, you see I am not thinking as excellently as the Lord. Now, more people are giving their lives away, more churches involved, relationships growing between the people of Southside and these mostly retired gentlemen. In fact, at a Christian business luncheon I heard one of these men give a list of the blessings in his life and right in that list was that once a month he goes to Sacramento to get food for the food bank at The Father's House.

Now we don't have to cover the cost of fuel and the man hours of getting the food. This is a job for someone who understands paperwork and has the patience for the people at the Gleaners. Just anybody cannot do this every Thursday. These very good people from this men's group have given their lives, saved the food bank, blessed our church immensely, and are an irreplaceable part of a "Jesus ministry."

I am always dreaming about projects to serve Oroville and tell the people of the city that Jesus loves them, that He sent us to tell them. Now the last thing that most of the people of Oroville or any other

American city want to hear, is that Jesus or anyone else loves them. At least that is their response to this love being verbal. So, when the interns from our Kingdom Awakening Apprenticeship school went out on their weekly outreach and set up a table with a sign saying free prayer and spiritual readings, I was in awe of their testimonies. People responded to these loving interns. I think people don't know what to do when Christians don't want anything from them and just give their time and energy to help them. We also have free car washes to raise money for the children's programs. What we do is get sponsors to sponsor the kids who will wash cars. We tell them that we are going to wash 100 or 120 cars for free and if they would sponsor us twenty five cents a car, it would be twenty five dollars. With a little effort you can raise fifteen hundred dollars in three hours of washing cars. This is great money for a car wash but what is more exciting is that the kids are not asking people to give them money for doing nothing. They can't quit until the quota is made in washing cars or they don't get the money.

We as a church get to say to one hundred and twenty car owner plus their passengers that we love them and Jesus sent us to wash their cars. We always want to tell them that we are getting paid by others to wash their cars and that we do not expect them to pay.

A free car wash is usually code for we expect donations. At these car washes it is hard to control what people say to the drivers when they talk to them on the side. The workers may tell them that we want donations, yet it is always The Father's House model to wash their cars for free. The donations that they make are supposed to be secondary and if getting donations takes away from our message that Jesus loves you, then getting a donation would take away the blessings that thirty or forty car washers would receive from giving their lives away. If this is the case then we have lost an awful lot to receive a few hundred dollars in extra donations. Instead we want to hold true to our assignment and operate in the opposite spirit of what we believe holds our city hostage, we want to operate in selflessness and wash cars as a service of love to the people of Oroville.

CHAPTER 22

Farming in the Garden

RECENTLY, I shared a long awaited dream that I had for a Father's House project. We would plow up the ground that we have and plant a huge vegetable garden. We would then give the vegetables away to anyone who comes, setting up tables on the highway with signs that read free vegetables and prayer. I did not know who could be that committed or who knew enough about vegetable gardening on such a large scale. This is not a job for the idealistic mind, this is a job to count the cost of.

This is what was on my mind when Rick approached me. I listened to his envisioning experience and heard his story that he wanted to go camping and gold mining with his family. When he heard me share my dream for the church farm, Rick said that he knew and felt the conviction of the Lord on him and he said to his wife, "that is my job, that is my calling."

We began the process of planning a garden. I knew that in ministry everybody thinks something sounds good, they sign up to help, then they find out that this sounded better than it feels. This is long hard work. After listening to Rick I knew that he had the right understanding of this project but that there would be a lot of wannabes who would promise to help and then fade out on him. I have felt this discouragement and I believed that he had the right attitude. Sure enough, he was out there by himself hour after hour, day after day. Then the help began to filter in. He was sacrificing days of pay on his job, nights at home with his family.

On planting day there was a car wash, a yard sale and planting day. I was at planting day installing the watering system and The Father's House showed up. I had to go to the hardware store several times and went by the car wash. There were thirty five people there giving their lives away to Oroville in the name of Jesus. I swung back by the yard sale and it was packed with customers and workers, this yard sale was not free, it was a benefit to keep someone out of jail. The other saints of LRM were laying down their lives to help someone avoid going back to jail while they were doing so well.

I have seldom been more proud of The Father's House Church! Fourteen thousand square feet of planting was done on that day with about fourteen more to be put in, in growing stages. Rick knows his stuff. He had flowers planted that naturally keep the insects down, he had flowers planted to help cause the bees to do their job. Who would have thought of this? Now I understand what he meant when he said to me, "pastor, this ain't my first vegetable garden," and it was not.

This could be the greatest thing that I have seen in my time of church leadership. Rick is a former alcoholic and drug addict. He has seen the underbelly of life. He has been a taker and now he is a giver extraordinaire. Rick is a world changer, a doer of the word and not just a speaker of it. Rick is a worshipper of Jesus and he has a revelation of God's love for him.

CHAPTER 23

But He Won't

WHEN I was a youth pastor, I had been associated with The International Church of the Foursquare Gospel for many years. I went to a kid's camp at the Foursquare youth camp in northern California called Old Oak Ranch near Sonora. The speaker at this camp was Karen Himebuck. We would gather as camp staff at night and have fun. The camp director had asked Karen to perform for us a sermon that she had memorized of Sister Amiee McPherson. She had memorized every inflection and every stutter and mistake as well as every word. Right there in that fireside room in that kids camp, on that day my life was changed.

Karen had obtained a tape of this message from the Foursquare archives. Karen even had a dress made, when she was talking she became Sister Amiee Semple McPherson, the founder of The International Church of the Foursquare Gospel and General in God's Army that legend has her to be. Amiees' sermon delivered by someone else some forty five years after her death is still one of the most powerful sermons that I have ever heard.

Karen began, and it went something like this, although I am doing this from memory and I don't wish to tarnish Karen's delivery or Sister's anointing. This is the part I want to recall to you.

"I was talking to a sister in our church who wanted to talk to me about planting a vegetable garden to help the people."

"But she said I don't know how to plant a vegetable garden."

"Well I know a man in our church who could plant a real nice garden, why he could plant any kind of garden and help the people. BUT HE WON'T."

"Now that got me thinking, I bet that there are people in our church who could do a real nice children's Sunday School or a real nice youth group, BUT THEY WON'T."

"I bet there are people who could afford to give the money (I don't remember the amount but it was not much) that it takes to put one of these young people through Life Bible College training and send them out to every nation preaching the Foursquare Gospel, BUT THEY WON'T." (My apologies to Sister for the inaccuracies).

If you are at all familiar with her ministry then you know that the words, THEY WON'T, and the things that the church could do if THEY ONLY WOULD, went on for a while. I was forever transformed.

Amiee, this woman preacher who had lost a husband on the mission field in China, who had been so innovative in the preaching of the gospel, as well as being a woman running such a large ministry in her day when there was so much opposition to woman leaders, had really hit me and inspired me to look at myself and decide just what it was that I would do.

Some things about Sister that not many people know is that she fed more people out the back door of the church than the county of Los Angeles welfare system. I believe she was in the newspaper every day for twenty years. There must have been a reporter assigned to Angelus Temple and Sister Amiee.

The Father's House Church and the city of Oroville, as well as the

Orsillo family, have been richly blessed by the ministry and example of Sister Amiee Semple McPherson and the International Church of the Foursquare Gospel. Many thanks to Karen for bringing this message to us at Old Oak Ranch, which is also one of Sister's legacies.

My friend Rick the farmer certainly will be used of God to do the work of the Gospel of Jesus. He would ruin Amiee's sermon but good, because "HE WOULD" and so would so many others at The Father's House. I am proud to serve along side of them.

Another element to Sister's ministry that made the heritage of Foursquare so rich for me is the power anointing that I see in her ministry. I look at Jesus' life, I hear Jesus' words that I should walk in the power that He secured for me.

Then when I look at Amiee's ministry, the doing of works of mercy, then the power evangelism that she ministered in, I feel in my spirit a sense that we are supposed to have this power in our ministries. If you wanted to see power in her day you would go to where she was preaching. Bring the sick, bring the broken hearted, she was full of grace and anointing. Giving out food by day and healing the broken hearted and afflicted by night.

This is the example of the ministry that I want flowing in my church. So, I pray for those who come to me. Many get healed, saved, filled with the Holy Spirit, they see visions and dream dreams, they feel, hear and see God. They worship Him with great love in spirit and in truth. They then pray for others and the same begins to happen.

This is not big stories for the newspapers, it is not big news, it should be everyday fruit of the Holy Spirit. If we can't have it here, or if doing things our way doesn't get it done, then let's move on until we can. We need to press in until we get it. We need to get enrolled With Christ in the School of Being Christian or just "Live and Love Jesus" until signs and wonders are following us. Until signs and wonders are evident wherever we have been.

This ministry of the sheep or this ministry of Jesus must be the focus of the church. Our testimonies must be about God's love and power. This power evangelism must accompany us wherever we go, so that people will know that God loves them and it is His pleasure to free them. The world will know that we are HIS disciples, because we have been set free and what we have received we will give to them in His name. This is the love that will reveal as Jesus said that we are His disciples, not disciples of religion.

God asks "who will go for me?" We must say "I will go for you."

Our answer to the requests that are brought to us that are Jesus' ministries should be "I WOULD," not "I WON'T."

CHAPTER 24

The Abundant Life

IT IS often asked of us, "how do you do it"? What we are being asked about is the large amount of things that we do. We pastor a church, own and operate a construction company, we own twenty four rental properties.

We have four children, these children are active in everything. They are honor roll students, athletes, actors, and very active in the church.

Nicole is a leader of leaders. She is very creative and inventive, she recently opened a business in event planning and decorations. Nicole is gifted beyond belief and always faithful.

Mark has Down's Syndrome and is the light in the world, Mr. Personality, he introduces us to every human alive. He reaches goals a great deal beyond his disability.

Danielle plays basketball for Arizona State University on a full ride scholarship, she was in Sports Illustrated recently, not for her basketball but for her work in the Tempe area with developmentally delayed adults.

Anthony is probably the most generous person that I have ever known. He is genuinely kind and has a servant's heart. Probably the one who is most like his mother.

They have all avoided the trappings of the world, they are drug free, committed virgins till marriage. They all love Jesus and have very anointed ministry in their lives.

Vicki and I are more in love after twenty nine years than we were on our wedding day. We spend more time alone together than most of the people we know. We actually use our boat, and spend a lot of time sitting on our deck visiting with family and friends. Our church has twenty one people on staff. The construction company recently had twenty two employees and fifteen subcontractors, working on between four to eight projects at all times.

When people ask how we do it, I know what they are asking, and my simple answer is that it seems easy. That answer does not warm their dear little souls. I am aware that this evidence of our lives can leave some feeling down or like they do not measure up. Maybe they just decide that we have some Samson anointing or some other supernatural thing going on. We do have a supernatural thing going on and if I give everyone the long answer, well I would spend a lot of time telling a lot of people this story.

On March 10th, 1975, I went forward at a Christian rock concert where the band Sweet Comfort was playing. At that time I hated Christians and did not want to be one. I never wanted to set foot in a church again. How I got to this concert was that I was visiting my brother in Stockton, California and he invited me to a rock concert.

In my life there had been times when I would pray, "I wish there was a way that I could go to heaven." So when the musicians shared about a personal knowing of God, that he wanted to know me, I went forward. I prayed with a guy by the name of Bryan Duncan, before we prayed I let him know that this was a waste of time, I could not change. Bryan asked that if God would change me would I let Him? I said "yes." Bryan asked, "if God would make Himself known to me, would I follow Him." I said "if He is real and He will change me, I will follow Him." I was set up. We prayed for no more than twenty seconds and when I opened my eyes the world was a different place! Air felt different, trees were a different color green, I do not know how else to explain it other than the world was changed and I was different. I was BORN AGAIN, made brand new. I now knew that He was real and more important was that He loved me. To coin a phrase from the card game Texas Hold Em, "I was all in". Right there and then I was "all in". I don't know any better way to describe it. Bible studies every night, more rock concerts, telling people everywhere I went that they could know Jesus in just twenty seconds of prayer.

I would park my car and hitchhike up and down the road just getting in people's cars to tell them about this miracle. Many would pray and everybody that prayed would cry and say, "I can't believe that it was so easy"! I would go skiing and leave my friends so that I could yell, "single", and get strangers on the chair lift up in the air. Many would pray, crying by the time we got to the top. They would thank me for showing them God's love, and helping them get forgiven.

I was, "all in," from day one, no education, no bible college, just "all in." My deal with God was "if you are real and you will change me, I will follow you." My first lesson was that it was Jesus I had prayed to, it was Jesus who said to the disciples, "follow me," it was Jesus who the Father said, "listen to him," it was Jesus that I needed to follow. As I said before, I was a Jesus man and I could not get enough of talking about Jesus. I could not get enough of hearing about Him either.

The changes in me, whew! I was a different person, no more drinking, cussing or smoking pot, it was all gone. Oh yes He was changing me and He was real to me. I had given Him my life.

The simple answer to the question, "how do you do it" is that I gave Jesus my life and never took it back. My days and my nights, my energy and my time, my money and my possessions, my marriage and my children, my ministry and my church, they all belong to him.

I do have a supernatural thing going on that is so much more powerful than healing a person's physical body, doctors can do that. It is that I am forgiven and that makes me eligible to be filled with the Holy Spirit. No man can do that. He gives me abundant life and that's how we do it. We just have a life filled with love and ministry, joy and peace, goodness and mercy. In addition to that, I lay my hands on the sick and they do recover. I also walk into the darkness and the light of God's kingdom lights up the darkness. That light moves obstacles and reveals God to a dying world.

The practical answer to the question "how do you do it" is that I have incredible people around me. If I told you about every detail of this organization and how it ran you might then wonder where we got these people. From the foreman on our jobs, to the office managers, the assistant pastors and the interns, there are the people in the church who step up to give their lives away. They run ministries that God has birthed in them. All I do is make myself available to help them when they need it. I promote people in the church based whether or not they are sons or daughters to The Father's House Church. I ask myself if they are "all in?"

What are the easy answers to the questions surrounding my endurance? Doing everything I do from my love for the Lord and appreciating everything He has done for me. Keeping Him as the Lord of my life and not wrestling control back because of worldly concerns. Keeping the throne of my life in order, Jesus on the throne, my wife second and my children third, with everybody else next and me bringing up the rear. I will have no idols or give the Devil any place in my life, as long as I practice the principle of giving my life away, my days and my nights, my energy and my time, my money and my possessions, my marriage and my children, as well as my church and my ministry; then they will all be abundantly blessed and "doing it all" will continue to be easy, not a burden to me or my family. Not one thing in this list will become an idol before my commitment to "follow Him." "Giving your life away," defined as, giving freely what has been given to you, is the secret to the abundant life. I have seen all the fads in Christianity come and go, as new revelations. I have lived through the salvation revival of the Jesus movement. I have been renewed in the Toronto Blessing. I would not change any of it. I have loved it all, The words of Jesus that if you "give it will be given to you, pressed down shaken together and running over" are not for the right time, they are for all times! They are the operating model for a life called Christian *"Freely it has been given unto you, freely give it away."* If you lack time, then give your time away. If you lack energy, then give what you do have away, do not hoard it to yourself. Is money the biggest problem that you face? Give what you have away, give from your need.

Does your life seem like the abundant life, the fulfilling of the promise in the words of Jesus? If you are not experiencing the promise contained in Jesus' words that you would *"have life and have it more abundantly,"* then give your life away for the benefit of someone else. You will begin to feel that your life is abundant and even the words, "it is easy," might be your answer to the questions that people ask about the supernatural nature of your life.

CHAPTER 25

The Riches of the Teachings of Jesus

IT SEEMS that no matter how long that I study the teachings of Jesus I never stop receiving life changing revelations from His teaching. A few years ago when we were at a conference at Harvest Rock Church in Pasadena, California, I listened to a sermon by John Arnott. John preached what I think was the beginning revelation of a message that I believe has become the most important message in Christianity today.

I don't understand why I did not get this revelation much earlier but I didn't. I was sitting in the church listening to John and I got real mad, to this day I have no idea why I got so mad, but I got mad. I did not get one thing out of this sermon, except that how could John say what he was saying.

The next time that I heard this sermon was under the mezzanine at

TACF in Toronto, Canada. I was floored, I have no words to describe the fact that I could not hear this truth the first time. On the second hearing it was the revelation of my life.

The message was called the "Importance of Forgiveness". I would have to say this has become the most important message for any Christian today. How had I missed it? There is one thing about the importance of forgiveness that must not be ignored. It is stated in the teachings of Jesus that if you do not pay attention to this principle, you will not avoid its consequences. I began to speak this message to my church about twice a year.

The following is a transcript of one of those sermons, which is part of our on-going study of the book of Luke.

We've been in the Lord's Prayer and we've talked about the disciples asking the question, "*Lord, teach us to pray.*" I had asked you on several occasions how often you ask of the Lord, "teach me to pray." Where does this request get placed in its priority in the prayers of your life? "Lord, teach me to pray." Learning how to pray, where is that in your priority structure? I'm letting you know that learning to pray really ought to be pretty high on our discipleship list.

The disciples, having seen Jesus and seeing that He prayed a lot, said, "*Lord, teach us to pray.*" What's funny, is that in the book of Matthew he says, "*Don't pray in vain repetitions, like the Gentiles do,*" yet the very statement He made about how to pray, we as modern Christians have turned into vain repetitions. So, it's not what you say or saying it the right way, but it's more about the content of what He taught.

In the book of Matthew the Lord's Prayer is much more expounded upon and in the book of Luke it's explained much less. Luke was going by the reports of people and Matthew was an eye witness.

Where we find ourselves today is probably the most important subject I know of in modern Christianity. It's the one most forgotten by many people.

In Luke chapter 11, verse 3: He had just finished saying, "*Your kingdom come,*" when He says, "*Give us each day our daily bread and forgive us our sins for we ourselves also forgive everyone who is indebted to us. And lead us not into temptation..."* This is the extent of what Luke records of Jesus' instructions on prayer. In it, He says, *"give us our daily bread and forgive us our sins."* Now a great many people break out the *"give us our bread"* as if it is different than *"forgive us our sins."* What *"give us our daily bread"* is, is much more important than what we call a loaf of bread made from different elements such as flour. In their day they had unleavened bread and leavened bread. Here Jesus uses the word bread to say, give us our daily needs. Jesus said, ask the Father to give you your daily bread. Well, man does not live by bread alone. So if you're really asking for provision, I wouldn't think very many of you would call bread alone provision. I believe that what Jesus was talking about and what most commentaries and commentators believe and the whole 2,000 year history of Christianity has been taught, is that *"Give us our daily bread"* really means, "Meet our needs, give us what it takes to follow You and survive." The next words are, *"Forgive us our sins as we forgive those who sinned against us."* Could it mean that to be forgiven and then forgive should be the *"daily bread"* that we pray for?

This is an interesting subject. In the book of Matthew He goes on to say, **"If you do not forgive, you will not be forgiven. This is how My Father will deal with you."**

He makes it the most important subject that you and I as Christians have ignored. We really have. The vast majority of us love the part about *"forgive me,"* but when we say "only as" or "just as," we're really saying "Give me what I want, only as I give You what you want." This ensures I get nothing I want if I'm not willing to give You what You want. "Forgive me only as I forgive," puts a condition on forgiveness that most of us ignore. It's like putting stuff on the charge card, never intending to pay for it. It really doesn't work out well in the end and neither will this.

There's a law in the Bible that begins right away in Genesis. Moses is called *"the lawgiver."* There's a verse that says *"the law has come to us through Moses, but grace and peace through Jesus Christ."* When I share this message, quite often people understand in their minds that there are two systems. There are two completely different systems and one of the mistakes made in Christianity is the attempt to live in both systems at once. The confusion that the world has about Christianity is caused by Christians trying to live under both covenants at one time. We want all the blessings of one covenant and not all the curses. We want all the blessings of the other covenant and not all the responsibility. We confuse Christianity until people don't want it because it's confusing, unapproachable, distasteful; it doesn't feel or sound good when we marry the two. These are two completely different systems.

One of them functions entirely and completely on justice: eye for an eye, tooth for a tooth, tit-for-tat. You did wrong and you pay the fine, you did wrong and you do the time. You hurt me so I hurt you. You hurt me and someone else hurts you. Paybacks are law. You do wrong out here and you run from the police because you know the payback for what you did is coming. You hide from the law. The law will exact from you what is required to pay your debt and more. This system is a good system. Our legal system is very much founded on it. It doesn't exactly run fairly because it's run by men, but it's a system of justice, and guess who created this system of justice? God. It's a wonderful, beautiful system. It ensures that you understand if you steal mine, there's a price to pay and someone will exact this price upon you. There's a certain comfort in it. You hurt me and I have the right to go to the law and get the law to hurt you back, making it so you might not want to injure me. Making it so you might think twice about climbing in the window at night and stealing and robbing and killing. That's the intention of the law of justice.

But Jesus came and created a different law, one called *"mercy and grace."* *"The law has come to us through Moses but mercy and grace has come to us through Jesus Christ."* Two completely different systems.... You can't have one in the other. You can't say, "I got mine, but I don't want you to have yours," or, "You hurt me and I want you to be injured. But, I hurt you and I want to be forgiven." That's the way I lived for a long time. "I want you to be hurt for what you did to me. I want you to pay for the wrongs you've done, but Lord, I ask you to forgive me and set me free from what I have done wrong."

Forgiveness, grace, and mercy is much better. I have lived in both systems and I'm here as an eyewitness to tell you: grace and mercy is better and that's what I want. I don't want to pay for my sins. Dad would grab the belt or Mom would say, "Go get the stick from behind the refrigerator," and I'd do anything I could to hide it, lose it, run out the door, "maybe he won't be as mad later." I don't want to pay for what I've done!

I really like going before the judge and having Jesus step up and say, "Father, I paid for his sins. I've covered them in the blood of the cross." I like that. It's a much better system.

Today we're going to look at how we try to live in both systems. "I want mine forgiven. I want you to pay for what you've done." If you want justice then you live where Satan shines. Wanting justice is like giving Satan a key to your house. It's like giving him the right to accuse. The Bible says he's the accuser, accusing the brethren all day long. I believe what he's doing is acting as the D.A. of the invisible realm. He's the accuser, the one that brings evidence that you and I have failed.

I may not know your secrets, but I know that I'm not very hard to convict. I'm guilty! So if you want to accuse me in the courtroom? I'm guilty! The witnesses can line up all day to say, "Yeah, we saw him. We know him." I haven't got a chance in this courtroom.

The Father is the judge. Now, if I was the accused, I'd throw myself on the mercy of the court. I can't prove myself innocent when I know I'm guilty. The accuser has all the cards. We do get to choose whether or not we want to be in the courtroom, where we don't have a chance in this law of justice. I know I don't have a chance in this court room, do you?

I only have one hope, that I would be purchased into the throne room of God where He would call me "son," where He would call me "beloved," where He would forget what I've done and cast it into the sea of forgetfulness, where He would remember my sins no more.

That's the only hope I have. That's the only hope you have. So what is my guarantee that I will be in the throne room and not the courtroom? If Jesus forgives me and my sins are seen and remembered no more. Luke quotes Jesus as saying, *"Do not judge and you will not be judged. Do not condemn and you will not be condemned. Pardon and you will be pardoned. Give and it will be given to you. They will pour into your lap a good measure, pressed down, shaken together, running over. For by your standard of measure it will be measured to you in return."* People quote this verse all the time relating it to money. Could it be any clearer that He's not talking about money? You can apply it to money but that's not what He was talking about. It's about judgement and forgiveness. Who's He talking to? You and me. Judge and you must be judged, not you might be judged or you could be judged. Judge and you *"will be judged."* That scares me! Forgive, judge not, and you won't be judged. That excites me! I was going into court with no chance and He said, "Wait a minute! All charges have been dropped!" "Give," He said, and what He's talking about is not money. Give forgiveness and *"it will be given to you, pressed down, shaken together, running over"* in abundance. I need this abundant forgiveness in my life.

I just had my 34th birthday of being born again, so I should be done with this stuff. Rebellion should be a past thing for me but it's not! Anger to the point of sin should be finished in me, but it's not. "Aren't you done renewing me yet Jesus?" I still need forgiveness. I still need to be on guard against judgement and unforgiveness because the accuser is there all day in the courtroom charging me with new charges. But over in the throne room my Father is saying, "What are you talking about? I have forgotten that".

James 2:13: *"Mercy triumphs over judgement."* I've been forgiven through grace, the unearned favor of God, I didn't accomplish a great feat of bravery to get it. I didn't have to be the knight and slay dragons to get it. I just got it through unmerited favor. I received forgiveness and so I have to give it as well. I have said things like, "Yeah, but he didn't do anything to deserve forgiveness. That guy didn't even ask for forgiveness, He didn't slay any dragons for me. He didn't build any buildings for me." If I want to put conditions on forgiveness, then I get conditions on mine. *"Mercy triumphs over judgement,"* is James the apostle's definition of this. Mercy will cancel out the law of justice. You won't have to pay, but make others pay and you will have to pay.

Matthew 18:23 *"For this reason the kingdom of heaven may be compared to a king who wished to settle accounts with his slaves. When he had begun to settle them, one who owed him 10,000 talents was brought to him; but since he did not have the means to repay, his lord commanded him to be sold, along with his wife and children and all that he had, and repayment to be made. So the slave fell to the ground and prostrated himself before him saying, 'Have patience with me and I will repay you everything.' The lord of that slave felt compassion and released him and forgave him the debt. But that slave went out and found one of his fellow slaves who owed him 100 denarii and he seized him and began to choke him, saying, 'pay back what you owe!' So his fellow slave fell to the ground and began to plead with him, saying, 'Have patience with me and I will repay you!,' he was unwilling and went and threw him in prison until he should pay back what he was owed. So when his fellow slaves saw what had happened, they were deeply grieved and came and reported to their lord all that had happened. Then summoning him, his lord said to him, 'You wicked slave. I forgave all the debt that you owed me because you pleaded with me. Should you not have also had mercy on your fellow slave in the same way that I had mercy on you?' And his lord, moved with anger, handed him over to the torturers until he should repay all that was owed him."* (If you get nothing else in the world, get this.) **"My heavenly Father will also do the same to you, if each of you does not forgive his brother from his heart. My heavenly Father will deal with you in this way."**

This is not a promise we're hearing third-hand. It isn't a very gifted preacher saying these words. This is Jesus, quoted by Matthew, he's an eyewitness, telling you that Jesus said, "*This is how My Father will deal with you.*" He said this right after telling a story that should blow everyone's minds. In fact, what I'm saying right now should blow your mind.

How many of you believe that the sins you've already been forgiven for can later on be put back on you and the punishment reinstituted? I doubt anyone would say "I do." If I hadn't read that scripture to you would you say, "No way! It's a sea of forgetfulness! As far as the East is from the West, He's forgotten them forever!" But, don't forget ,He's God. If I've forgotten them forever, maybe you can count on the fact that I'll never remember them. But this promise and this story is about a man who was forgiven and released, and then re-charged and punished for the debt he was already forgiven. That ought to scare us into saying, "Lord, who have I aught against? Who have I forced to repay? Who have I demanded justice from?" I don't want justice. I know me; I cannot survive justice. It won't go well with me in a world of justice.

The Father called me son, Jesus called us friends. These gather with the King in the Royal Palace. I must find myself in the throne room. I must find myself in forgiveness and the law of mercy and grace. I must not be found in the law of Moses. I must not find myself in the courtroom of justice. I must find myself in the throne room of grace and mercy. I must.

"So, Lord, tell me, who have I judged? Who do I still have aught against? Who do I still want to see punished?

He'll get his. Just wait until he faces God. He hurt me bad, but wait until he faces God. He'll get his then." I have said all of these things, have you?

Every time I share this message I'm aware that there are people in the crowd that have wounds that are huge, and who say, "I can't forgive. I can't. You don't know what that man did to me." Almost every time I speak this message someone looks at me and says, "This is hard, you don't understand."

First, I beg your indulgence but I'm just telling you what Jesus said.

Second, I know it's hard. A man may tell me, "You don't understand. I watched them kill my kids and then charge me with the murder. I'll never forgive them! What can I do?"

A women may say, "you don't know what he did to me. I was a helpless little girl, I'll never forgive him."

First you have to define what forgiveness is. Then you have to forgive. When the disciples said, *"Teach us to pray,"* Jesus said, *"Pray this: 'forgive me only as I forgive,' and "Why do you judge or try to get the speck out of your brother's eye instead of working on the log in your own eye?"* These are Jesus' words.

I want to live in the throne room, not the courtroom. I want grace for my sins. I don't want law; I want to be forgiven.

In Exodus 20, God says the sins of the fathers will be visited on the sons for generations and generations. Some of the curses that are transferred to the sons, the Bible says they will be transferred up to ten generations. The sins of the fathers will be visited upon the sons for up to ten generations.

I cannot afford to be in the courtroom, charged for what my grandfathers did. I have grandfathers who were some of the most evil men on earth. I cannot afford the effects of their sin.

I must be found in the throne room of God. I must come to the cross and the mercy seat. Jesus made it clear but we have ignored it. "I must be forgiven."

"But what about your dad and how he hurt you?" "Oh, he's gonna' pay." Then you cannot be forgiven. You cannot. Don't ignore Jesus any longer. Don't ignore what He says.

"This is how My Father will deal with you." Don't ignore it any longer. The first time I heard this message I was so angry but had no idea why. Today, this message is the most important message in my life.

I know a lot of you are experiencing turmoil in response to this message because there are some horrid things that have happened to you. Men have inflicted horrible things upon each other.

We have to come to terms with the definition of forgiveness if we want to be found in the throne room of God. We must not ignore the words of Jesus. They are absolute. If they have to pay, I have to pay.

Some people believe that forgiveness equals forgetting. If I haven't forgotten, then have I forgiven? I do not believe this. Do you then let the child molester run the children's program? Of course you cannot forget. A simple definition of forgiveness is, "I don't want them punished for what they did to me."

Let me give you an example: Stephen being stoned saw heaven and said, Father, don't let one man be judged for murdering me.

Abel: The Bible says that to this day Abel's innocent blood is crying out for justice against his brother Cain. Innocent blood crying out for justice will have an incredible generational affect for years to come and many people will have to pay.

Jesus on the cross said, "Father, forgive them." Guess what? There will be no one in hell for the sin of murdering Jesus. They might be in hell for the sins and the life they choose. That's not our call. I can't get anyone to heaven. All I can do is make sure that no one goes to hell for what they did to me.

I know the pain that's growing inside of some of you right now. I've been through forgiveness for a certain individual at least 20 times. Two days ago I went through it again; I just wanted to make sure. "Father, forgive that man. When he stands before You, let him go. I'm OK. Don't judge him for how he hurt me. Forgive him." That man will stand before God and give an answer for his own life and I have no joy in that. I pray that he would be saved.

But recently I was writing an article and had to tell the story of my wounding by this individual and I realized I was pretty free. The first time I remembered it, I was 30 years old and I murdered this man in my mind. I sat through red light, green light, red light, green light, as I, with incredible tentacles of hate and misery, hated him so much that I killed him viciously in my mind. When I opened my eyes and all the cars were honking at me and my car was completely fogged with water dripping inside from the incredible sweating of my intensity, I said, " Lord there's something wrong with me. I need help." Had he been on the street I would have used my strength against him. Win, lose, draw, I was crazy.

The result of my anger toward this man showed up on a day when my daughter was being treated unfairly by a coach. The person who wounded me happened to be a coach also and I made a vow that I'd never let my children be treated unfairly by a coach. I was at a Christian school basketball game under the impression that this man had been unfair to my daughter. My wife had me by the tail of my shirt being dragged across the floor while my other daughter was grabbing my arm, pulling me, as I tried to get across the floor. I had no idea what I was mad about, but I was under the curse of the law. I had judged the first man so desperately and had hated him for so long, I had forgot how much I hated him. I forgot how much I attributed my dreams being lost to him. I had forgotten all these things. I had no idea why I was such an idiot when it came to coaches being unfair to my children. I had to ask why was I out of control?

In counseling, people say things like, "I'll never be like my father! He abused me. He was an alcoholic. I'll never marry anyone like him!" Then they marry a man who's nothing like him but two or three years later he's exactly like him!

A man says, "I hate my father. He hit us. He beat my mother all the time." They hate him yet find a rage inside them trying to come out, and it makes them just like him.

When I judge others, there's a law going on. There's a rule going on in the world that if I judge them, I get the consequence of what I judge. A measure is being measured out to me. It is the measure that I used.

But if I will give mercy because I want mercy, I will then say, "Lord, forgive them, do not punish them for what they did to me, let them go Lord." Go ahead and give them a gift they don't deserve. You can even say they don't deserve it. Some people say if you say, "That hurt me, that changed my life," then you haven't forgiven. I can tell you that shortly after I went through prayer for the coach who wounded me, I walked through a gymnasium and for the first time in my life the high school coach walked over to me, sat down and said, "Hey, what do you think is wrong with my team?" "You're asking me?" Coaches always stayed as far away from me as they could. This forgiveness changes the world.

People come to me wanting to be different, saying things like "I feel like I'm in a current. I'm being dragged a certain way. I can't stop who I am. I can't stop what I'm doing."

The first question I always have is, "Is there somebody who comes to your mind that you need to forgive, or who's injured you badly? Do you think "I hate that man" when you think of anyone? You may try to put it under the blood and say, "No, I love everybody," trying to wash it away and stuff it down. "Let's talk about your dad." "Oh no, I don't talk about him."

There are warriors here today who have had friends killed, mutilated, and tortured. There are people here who have faced war.

There are men and women here today who have faced an amazing amount of abuse, who have been slapped around, beaten, and molested. I am so deeply sorry those things happened to you. It makes me cry to think about them. When I hear them I am so proud of who you are today, how you've made it through the kind of pain you've made it through, to even show up in a church like this today, and how you have survived in the face of some of the things you've survived in.

But I cannot then say, it's okay to not face it. I want to see you in heaven and the Word says you cannot be forgiven if you do not forgive. The answer to the prayer, "Lord, teach me to pray," is this: "Forgive me, only as I have forgiven."

Jesus goes on to say, "*You will not be forgiven if you don't forgive.*" You will not be able to escape judgement if you continue to judge.

The wicked manager says, "*I'm unable to pay.*" My sins are many, and he is forgiven.

My abuses may be minor compared to some of yours, but they enslave me just the same. I'm unable to pay, Lord.

He took the bread and He told them, I will be broken for you. If you'll take the bread, if you'll take the wine, you'll be forgiven, if you will forgive, Jesus said, I will purchase for you new, abundant life. I will help you to become sons and daughters of My Father. I will prepare a place for you. I will sanctify you. All of this is offered to you and me for free.

The first time I heard this message I was irate and out of control. If it's making you mad, I'm certainly a person who understands that.

The second time I heard this message wasn't very long ago and that time I fell on my knees and said, "Oh God, how could I have preached your word for all these years and been so deceived? How did I miss this? I have hated so much while I have loved so much. How did I miss this?"

So I asked Him, "Lord, if there's anyone out there whom I haven't forgiven would you show them to me?" There must have been two hundred of them! For the next month and a half I couldn't go to the store, stop at a stop sign, or a stoplight, or walk around a corner without running into one of these people. This was followed by a pregnant pause, an uncomfortable feeling, my breath taken away.

Then they'd walk by and I'd say, "Hey, wait a minute. Do you remember when we had that fight over Little League? ...or we had that argument? Remember when our kids got into a fight and we haven't been friends since?" Two hundred of these experiences!

I'd be sitting at a stoplight and look at the car to my side, see someone who I needed to forgive and have to pray. "Lord, I ask that You make sure they are forgiven for the wrong they did me. Let them go. Forgive them. When they stand before You make sure they're not judged for that." A prayer like that is just the housecleaning. I still need to ask for forgiveness for judging them.

A lot of us have wounds that control us and so we need to ask God to show us. Some of the wounds may be so hard to deal with that you need another to help you through it. We're glad to do that. That's our main job as Christians. Jesus does the forgiving. We just help you identify it.

Begin to pray and if you have a place in your life where you're out of control, ask God. Define forgiveness as letting those who've hurt you go and you'll find out it's much easier than saying what they did was right. You know as well as I do what they did wasn't right. It hurt you badly. You're not over it. It still hurts, it still wounds. You are where you are because of what they did to you.

Put it all in the basket. "Yes, you hurt me. Yes, you wounded me. Yes, you destroyed me. Yes, I am in a screwed up life because of you." Say it, get it out of you. "But now I'm gonna' ask my Father to forgive you and not punish you because of what you did to me." That's the definition of forgiveness if you define it correctly. Give the basket to Jesus.

God doesn't say that what we did was right. He doesn't say that what we did didn't hurt our world. He doesn't say that what we did didn't hurt our children. In fact, if you lived a crappy life and then you ask for forgiveness, your children are still affected by it. The outcome is still there. When you're forgiven all you are is forgiven.

Now you have to start the work of the restoration of the lives around you. All you're doing in forgiving your brothers and sisters is not wanting them harmed for having harmed you. Your fathers, your mothers, your neighbors, your coworkers, your Little League teams, etc., to the ends of the earth.

Father, teach me who I have aught against, that I might forgive them. We've been forgiven a huge debt. We say to the Lord, "We can't pay," and He says back to us, "Then go your way. Be forgiven. Your sins are forgiven you. *Go and sin no more.*"

We've spent a lot of time talking about "only as I forgive those," but there's a real important part about being forgiven. We say, "Father, forgive me". I don't want to be in the law that Moses taught. I want to be in the grace and peace that Jesus brought. Remember what Jesus said about forgiveness: "*Go and sin no more.*" He never planned to forgive people and let them keep doing what they're doing. He always intended that forgiveness would change you and transform you and cause you to be "*born again,*" brand "*new creatures in Christ.*"

Now let's pray and ask the Father to reveal to us if there is anyone who we need to forgive.

Just as Jesus saying "*love one another as I have loved you*", is the evidence that we are his disciples, this forgiveness is how the world will know it.

Forgiveness is the condition that is required for us to be forgiven. There is no way around this.

In my opinion this is the most important message for our time. Thank you John Arnott and thank you Jesus for this incredible revelation.

CHAPTER 26

The Hidden Harvest

THERE IS an old story that has become one of my favorites. It is not mine but I sure appreciate who ever told it first.

In a region somewhere in the midwest of the United States there were many beautiful farms, the land was rich and the water good, but there was one piece that no one ever farmed.

One day a man came to town to buy a farm, but there were none for sale.

The realtor said that there was this one piece of ground that he could buy but it was full of rocks and roots and no one had ever tried farming it. The man bought this land and he began to clear the trees and dig the rocks while he pulled the roots. He continued to dig and burn and burn and dig, until he was ready to plant. As time went on he built a home and other out buildings such as barns and corrals and he made even his fences beautiful until one day it was realized that he had the most beautiful farm in the region.

The people driving through began to stop and take pictures. Then others began to come to the town to see this farm.

One day as the man was working his fence line a car pulled up alongside and rolled down the window, the driver asked, "Sir do you know who owns this beautiful farm?"

The man answered, "I do." The driver said, "well the Lord sure has blessed you with a most beautiful farm."

The man said, "WELL YOU SHOULD HAVE SEEN IT WHEN HE HAD IT TO HIMSELF."

That phrase always sucks the air out of a room; you watch the faces of the people as they try to figure out if you were disrespectful to the Lord or not.

You should have seen my life when God was the only one who wanted me to be saved, healed and delivered. My life was not saved, healed, or delivered at that time.

It is always God's will to heal and save and deliver but it is not always done. But if somebody will dig and burn then water and build, then the life that is possible, (just like the farm that is overlooked, just like the life that is looked beyond or thought to be too much work), will flourish.

Just like the fig tree in Luke 13. "Let's dig around it give it some fertilizer and give it a chance then if it will not bear fruit then we can cut it down."

Many of the people that are real testimonies to the Lord's great love for the "supposed unlovable" are just like this fig tree. Too much work and they are not bearing fruit so get rid of them.

Joe came to us from jail and had been addicted to everything including methamphetamine and gambling. As a young boy about twelve he became associated with a service station mechanic who introduced him to how much money one could make selling drugs at the local school.

He is now in his forties and has seen a lot of water go under that bridge, literally, having lived as a homeless man for three years under a bridge eating out of garbage cans. Conning and stealing, robbing and hurting people with absolutely no fear or conscience. Addicted to all kinds of drugs, taking them in every form including the use of needles. Joe was addicted to gambling and all in all, just had a lousy attitude toward people in general. Joe's worst addiction was selfishness, and he serviced that addiction with reckless abandon.

Joe came to us three years ago. He spent a year in our recovery program, a year as you might guess that was full of conflict and introspection.

Joe had to be transformed from a taker into a giver and I've had the privilege of hearing his testimony. He had to have people around him who were trustworthy, or worthy of his trust and he was looking very close and judging very hard. It just so happens that many of the sons and daughters of God who live and work at The Father's House did not let him down. We were imperfect and yet very patient. We were willing to love Joe as the medicine for his predicament. When he was cussing a group of ladies in the alley and throwing a fit, it felt a lot like pulling roots and rocks!

He began to change and he applied to our intern and ministry apprenticeship program. A year in the servant role, daily laying down his life as a ministry house leader, began to have an effect on Joe as he became a son to his Father.

Joe is a brightly converted son. He runs our homeless outreach taking food, clothing, water, coats, blankets and sleeping bags to the homeless people in our area. He prays for them and tells them of a better life that God has for them. He also runs our maintenance and community service workers program. It is his third year in this ministry and just the other day he sat down to tell me that his goal is that his name be added to in the future. He wants his name to be Pastor Joe. He wants to be ordained to minister the Gospel of love and remain on our staff as a trainer and servant of the Father's love.

Joe is a world changer and a son. He is a 'brightly converted', "born again" lover of God's people, and I am very proud of him. You should have seen his life when God was the only one who wanted him blessed, saved, healed and delivered.

Joe has been confronted with a new way of living and he seeks God to help him every day and just when he is getting it, the old ways and the old man jumps up to take him down, but he says, "no I have to rest in God's love and return to the Lord's presence." He has worked through many struggles with himself and the old life that still exists. (I imagine that it feels a lot like pulling roots and rocks to Joe also.) The old life that keeps coming up is one he created in 40 years of wrong living and wrong habits. Like the struggles his children go through that he can't fix by his own right decisions, Joe must be willing to continue to work at the fruit of his life. His children are watching and he is investing in their future by showing them the way.

Joe is giving his life away, and in every life you "*give and it will be given to you.*" Joe is giving his life away for others and is in agreement with what God wanted for him since the day that he was born. Now God has a partner in the work of giving Joe an abundant life.

If no one ever begins to pull at the roots and invest in the future beauty of what God has placed in every life, if no one digs and burns and fertilizes the root system of life and the abundant life that God has breathed into every soul that was born in unfair circumstances, then will there ever be a harvest of the richness of life that is Devin, Louie, Kylee, Katie, Bob, Dave or Joe?

CHAPTER 27

You Should Have Seen it When God...

MY WIFE Vicki is the co-pastor of our church and has for many years been praying with people and helping them receive the healing in their hearts that they need. So at one point several years ago she began to develop a style of "inner healing" that was very simple and is based on the words of Jesus that if you *"judge then you will be judged, forgive and you will be forgiven."* Very simple words yet in most of our lives they are simply ignored and disregarded. People just believe that if they don't think about it then it probably doesn't affect them.

Some think that God will work on it by himself and that it will be beautiful even if they don't listen to His very direct words *"do not forgive and you will not be forgiven."* To do this really is like giving the devil a key to your house. What Vicki does is help people sit still and listen to God as He tells them where the problem in their life is and when it started. If they are open then it usually brings up emotions that surround the event in their life when they were hurt. She then leads them through prayers of forgiveness both for those that hurt them and sometimes God for allowing it to happen. Then they ask for forgiveness for their judgements and very quickly what had seemed like the devil's hold on them, or the prison that held them "*until they paid every cent of their debt*" seems to disappear and they are truly set free. Free to then work on the fruit bearing garden of their life.

You see, God always wanted to dig and burn at the roots and rocks in our lives but we would not believe Him that our judgements and unforgiveness could cause us to be unfruitful and imprisoned. Being set free from the effect of judgement and unforgiveness begins the process, now you have work to do in agreement with the Holy Spirit. Agreement that the Father loves you, that He has a plan for you that is for good and not for evil, that you really can hear God's voice and you can feel his presence around you. With this knowledge and revelation you will be able to break free from the bondage of sin's hold on you.

So many people testify that they really could not ever get past their own weaknesses until they began to let God show them what was happening in the spirit. How their wounds and offenses were holding them hostage and the Great Hostage Negotiator could not set them free until they set others free. Then they would be able to win against a very beatable enemy.

As long as unforgiveness and judgement are in our lives you will be subject to the cost of your sins and weaknesses. You will be subject to the words of Jesus "*this is how my Father will deal with you if you do not forgive,*" and "*until they paid every cent of their debt,*" you will stay in jail till you pay every cent.

I have lost the struggle with weight loss for many years and I want God to help me and in fact He wants to. In inner healing sessions with my wife we try to let God tell us where the root is. We want to identify every tentacle of the root that we can so that we forgive every offense and can be forgiven every judgement. When the root is gone I still have to say no to the bad foods if I want to lose weight and have the battle be winnable and not hopeless. I still have habits that I have to change.

The *"no temptation has overcome you"* seems more true than it did when the fruit of my unforgiveness was weakness. The fruit of my giving forgiveness was my own forgiveness which results in me having the righteousness of Jesus and the fruit of the Holy Spirit. Which is self control.

I actually have access to a life full of God's powerful gifts and fruit, it is certainly available to anyone who *"believes,"* and I do believe, but in my life I have lost many battles as a person who believes in being an overcomer living a victorious life. In the battle for weight loss I have been less than victorious.

Now I am free from the law of sowing and reaping and I can actually have a choice whether I will eat or not. If I will dig and burn at the rocks and roots in my life, I will have the life that God wanted me to have when he was the only one that wanted me to look like him.

People do say to me, "God sure has blessed you with a beautiful life." I must reply, you really should have seen it when He was the only one who was willing to work on it and die for that outcome.

If I am not willing to let God show me who I have judged or who I have not forgiven, then the Christian life does not have the power that I have always heard that it should have.

If I am unwilling to work out my own salvation with fear and trembling, unwilling to see the life that is in that soil and the beauty that is hidden underneath all that brush, expecting that it will just take care of itself and all those years of unhealthy habits do not need any resistance, then time will pass and the fruit that was bred into my DNA will not ever grow. It will never be partaken of by others. I will really be like a *"lamp put under a basket."*

The Christian life is a constant work. A work of seeking God who is easy to find. A work of learning his word, and since I love Him I do want to know His word, and live it, doing the works. It is a work of *"go and sin no more."*

Mostly it is the work of doing what Jesus said, "*loving one another as I have loved you.*" I could work on that one for the rest of my days. It is enough work just to learn how He has loved us, not just the cross either. I need to work at the good Samaritan kind of "*love your neighbor.*". The dig and burn, burn and dig, "thars gold in them thar hills" kind of love. In finding how deep is His love for me, I will find out how deep is my love for others. The one will show the other.

Allowing God to dig in your heart and reveal the hurts and judgements is this kind of work. This love that we are to have is revealed through His love for us. His love for us is seen in the forgiveness and grace that He gave us. His condition is that we forgive and love as we have been forgiven and loved. The work that is necessary is to let God dig in the garden of your heart. It hurts for a moment and then comes freedom. It is God's will that you be healed, heart, mind and soul, healed. Then you will be able to walk out your destiny and "*work out your salvation with fear and trembling.*"

CHAPTER 28

It is Good to Heal this Man on the Sabbath

IN LUKE chapter 14 Jesus is in a Pharisee's house when He sees this man who needs healing. So He asks, *"is it lawful to heal on the sabbath?"* Well they don't answer. *"And He took hold of him and healed him, and sent him away."*

Jesus then begins to tell them again how they would free their ox from a ditch but they won't free this man. You get the idea that they value an ox above a man. I believe they have some "stinkin thinkin" going on here.

How did they come to think like this? There is seven times in the Gospels that Jesus heals a person on the Sabbath. I get the impression that He really wants His people to understand that the rules were not to imprison people but to free them.

Yet, the rules and laws as the Pharisees enforce them are not about the love of people, but about a system. They have created a place for themselves as the obeyers of the law and since this is where they get their power and authority, this is what is important to them. It is as if they cannot hear Jesus as seven times He shows them the love of God by freeing, healing and showing great mercy on the sabbath. In this story the Pharisees' have Jesus over for lunch and it says that they were "*watching Him.*" They are not trying to build Him up or support His work, they are trying to catch Him. These men want something to use to destroy Jesus and prove to the people that once again they are the ones protecting the people from lawlessness and demonstrating righteousness.

Knowing this, Jesus asks them a question which requires them to decide, "*Is it good to heal this man on the sabbath?*" Then Jesus does heal him. So the answer is, it is good!

Today, in various churches and cities I hear discussions that are similar. People trying to discredit someone by questioning their actions or motives with questions that have nothing to do with the truth, questions like "what will people think" or "will people get the wrong impression"? Making statements like "and He calls himself a Christian". All in pretty much the same spirit that the Pharisees used to "*watch Jesus.*" People are afraid that their idea of what is right is being challenged so they begin to try to "catch" the person and discredit them, creating a place of honor for themselves and trying to raise their stature on the idea that the person with a different thought has done something wrong. Making themselves out to be the right one and the other person out to be wrong. The age old practice of getting to the top not by achievement but instead by pulling the other person down. Speaking from a self-righteousness instead of a righteousness based on grace. A grace that they have received, loving their neighbor as they have been loved.

Pharisees are still around today doing exactly the same thing because they were operating then with a spirit of religion and there are the same spirits leading people today to operate in the same manner as they did in Jesus' day. If people are doing this to you, then find comfort in the fact that they did it to Jesus as well.

If you are doing this to people then find comfort in the words of John the apostle when he wrote, "*if we sin, we confess our sin and the blood of Jesus cleanses us from every unrighteousness.*" Forgiveness is just a prayer away and in that we should rejoice exceedingly. For we have, "*all sinned and fallen short of the glory of God.*"

CHAPTER 29

The Robbing of Honor

IN THE story of Jesus having lunch at the Pharisee's house in Luke's 14th chapter, Luke says that they were "*watching Him.*" Trying to catch Him at make some mistake with which to discredit Him.

The action of pretending to be a friend or sitting in a church "*watching*" or just gossiping about the pastor, is hurtful and destructive in any sense but it is much more than that. In the stories of the Pharisees watching Jesus the Pharisees are trying to destroy Jesus not just discredit Him.

In the verse "*the devil comes to steal, kill, and destroy,*" there is a lot more implied in "*destroy*" than first meets the eye. The word 'destroy', is like the word 'kill'. It sometimes sounds like he wants to kill and kill you, but I don't think that makes much sense. I thought that there must be more to this word 'destroy', and there is. The word is more like remove any memory of you, or cause people to forget you. No heritage, no lineage, no evidence that you meant anything or even existed. Wow!

What is the purpose in that? Well, if you want a certain message to lose its power then you must destroy the messenger. If you watch anyone closely enough they **will not** disappoint you. They will make mistakes that you can discredit them with. If you try hard enough you can even rob them of honor. Then it can be as if they did not exist. The next time someone comes with their message the people say "we have heard that before and it did not work out so well." Dishonor is probably the best definition of that word 'destroy' that I have heard.

So if the devil comes to destroy honor and remove the message by discrediting the messenger, it seems that this would demand an answer to the question, "what is honor?"

I believe that honor is a gift that a person gives to themselves. When a person's actions are dictated by a code of behavior or are defined by *"loving your neighbor as Christ has loved you,"* then that person has given their life honor. You could say that they have become honorable. They have given themselves a gift. Their honorable life gives their words credibility.

We have a practice at The Father's House of honoring people. At a birthday party, any celebration or even just when someone could use it, we take turns saying what it is about the person's character, actions or message that have enriched our lives or inspired us to be better people. We call this honoring.

When broken down it is actually just saying that this person's actions in life have been noticed and valued. Mostly, it would be what the person has chosen to become and how it has blessed us. It is the honor that the person gave to themselves by being diligent or honest or just standing in the love of God. It could be that they are so loving. Even that is their choice and their gift to themselves.

Honor truly is a gift that a person gives to themselves. Honoring is when people recognize these gifts as a blessing and tell about it, both to themselves and the people around them, thus *"giving honor where honor is due."* First, you give yourself the gift of honor then others who recognize this applaudable gift begin to speak about it, spreading the message of virtue to others. When word gets around of this honor then the message of the honoree becomes more and more valid. When dishonor gets around then the message is discredited!

In our case it is the message of love, acceptance and forgiveness. In the world's case it is the destruction of our opponent. Like in politics, you cannot just disagree, it seems that you have to dishonor your opponent to win.

In the church the saddest part of dishonoring is that most of the dishonoring comes from within the body. It is the Pharisees that are "watching" so as to catch us at something, even to the point of agreeing with the enemy and coming to destroy.

When the world comes to battle us then the battle lines are clear, such as "the separation of church and state," that we are struggling with in the U.S. When faced with the loss of our freedoms to express our beliefs, we know what we have to lose because there are savings, healings and deliverances to be had and the fruit of waging the war of the spirit is *"fruit that remains."* If the struggle of the battle is an attack against our honor, and we are proven or even assumed to be dishonorable, then who would listen to us? Look at what is at stake. We in the U.S. have lost much because of the dishonorable behavior of so many who profess the cross of Jesus. It is hard to un-ring the bell that sounds so loudly through our land when the accusations of those who would oppose our message are true. Ministers who shout about sin caught in their own accusations, the killing of abortion doctors, the signs that are held high for all to see that say that God hates people who practice homosexuality.

We have to decide (I think), what team are we on? The *"save, heal and deliver"* team that accomplishes honoring or the *"steal, kill and destroy"* team that dishonors?

I have no problem with the verses like *"do not even associate with the immoral brother"* or *"turn him over to the devil for the destruction of the flesh"* verses because taking both of these actions is for the purpose of saving the individual who is *"turned over"* or *"not associated"* with from the deceiver, convincing them to repent or turn around. They have given themselves the gift of dishonor and are involved in their own destroying. If I let them continue in the sheepfold then I am participating in their dishonor and the dishonoring of our message. It is my greatest wish to save them. I am not doing it to be seen defending some cause. I am doing it to try and follow the teaching of the Apostle. If I can cause their repentance or their turn around then I have caused their honor. I have helped them give themselves a gift of honor, making them honor-able. Not taking action leads to lethargy and complacency which as we know is like leaven, and then spreads to others.

I have no problem dispensing love of this kind and trying to save *"the immoral brother,"* protecting them from causing their *"brother to stumble,"* therefore putting them in danger of the *"millstone around their neck and being cast into the sea"* ending to their dishonoring of themselves.

Saving, healing and delivering is tricky business if we forget to stop stealing, killing and destroying, if we continue dishonoring people and watching them to catch them doing something wrong.

Saving, healing and delivering gets easier when we remember to give ourselves the gift of honor then watch people for the purpose of catching them at doing good, and *"give honor where honor is due."*

CHAPTER 30

Who Am I?

IN THE story of Jesus having lunch at the Pharisee's house, one of the guests at this house spoke up and tried to sound wise. He wanted to say something that was relevant. I have been in this exact situation, talking to people who have taken on the religious or Pharisee role. They completely distract you from the point of what you were saying. If you try to get your point back on track, they will be uncomfortable. If you succumb to the feeling of discomfort, then the truth that needs to be heard, the truth that God has sent you to speak, gets left unsaid and the Pharisee's spirit of religion has won the battle. The guy who needs healing does not get healed.

Then Jesus replies with a story, He told them a story about a man who gave a dinner and invited many people to attend and they responded with excuses each one different than the other. He said, "*Go out at once into the streets and lanes of the city and bring in here the poor and crippled and blind and lame.*" The man told his servants to go out and invite others, but the servant told him that there was still room. *"And the slave said, Master, what you commanded has been done, and still there is room."* Then he invited the passers by from the *"byways and hedges"* that we always hear about, *"and the master said to the slave, 'go out into the highways and along the hedges, and compel them to come in, so that my house may be filled."*

Obviously this story is about the Jews not coming to the Lord's covenant or salvation and by not coming they have proven that they don't really know Him. It is also clear that they don't understand who they are to have received such an incredible privilege. Because they don't come to Him others are invited and I am sure glad of that because I am a *"highways and hedges"* invitee!

Jesus goes on to tell this story after asking the question about whether it is good to heal this man, revealing to them the truth that they would save their ox but be offended if this man were set free. Their understanding of God's love for people was screwed up. They thought He was all about the rules. Then He tells this story. It is a story of the invited guests that will be left out and other guests will be invited in their place. Not special guests but whoever just happens to be in the *"highways and hedges."* Not royalty or people of position like the ones He had just told them about before the man made his statement. Not people who one could benefit from but people who probably would be a cost to you, like the *"blind and lame,"* the *"poor and crippled."*

I read the Bible and I always stop myself from just going on and reading the next story, just receiving what I have always received. I stop and ask questions of myself and God, like, "Lord what do you want me to get from this story?" Thoughts come to my mind asking **who am I** in this story? I have always believed that I am the "highways and hedges" invitee, but who else might I be? Am I the one giving a dinner and the guests will not come? They always have excuses. Or am I the guest who always has excuses? Maybe I am the servant sent to invite the guests, who are to replace the guests, who have all the excuses. Or the *"blind and lame,"* *"poor and crippled"* outcasts who are invited to replace the original guests.

Could I be the *"highways and hedges"* person who was invited because there is plenty of room? The obvious answer is, I am a man who is invited to the feast of knowing God. I was given grace, I was not deserving. God chose to invite me, to even *"compel"* me to come to Him. Being included in the guest list means that I have access to God and qualify for all that comes with this invitation. All I have to do is answer that call and come.

Could I be the guest who sent his regrets on why he could not come? Have there been times when I had excuses why I could not come or be the guest that I am supposed to be?. There is always something very important that gets in the way like *"worrying about tomorrow."* I pray with all of my heart that this is not who I am.

I definitely am the servant who is sent to *"compel"* the *"highways and hedges"* people to come taste and see; they are invited to a most wonderful feast, an abundant feast. A servant, I definitely am, sent by my master with the great privilege of carrying His invitation.

You know people don't always like it when I invite them. They say that they have "been there and done that." I can relate to their opinion, since some of the feasts that I have been invited to have been all about hype. Someone telling me that it is wonderful, instead of me tasting and seeing for myself and finding out that it is good. The effort that some people who invited me to feasts put into their feast was not very good and some of them told me it was God's feast. He did not look like He had anything that I liked at His feast. People want to know where is the abundance that He promised anyways? I want to be the servant who simply demonstrates the presence of the Master to those who attend His abundant feast.

I am really found all over this story, I could be any one of these people. At times I am all of these people.

In the end the real meaning is the best, that the Father is throwing a banquet and He is going to invite me. If I accept, there will be a place for me. That place will be a place of honor if I give myself that gift. Those who did not attend did not receive what the Father had prepared for them. Those that did, received an abundance that *"eye has not seen, ear has not heard, nor has the mind of man conceived."*

Who am I? I have been them all, and who I am in the end will be exactly who I choose to be. The title of Son has been offered to me, I think I will choose that one.

CHAPTER 31

I Found It

AS THE servant *"sent to compel them,"* I was once involved in the "I found it" campaign, which really was a *"compel them to come in"* effort that I still think was brilliant. It was a billboard and media message that said "I found it". The person who was curious was supposed to call the toll free number to find out what you found.

"New life in Jesus Christ" was the answer and if you wanted to know more we would pray with you to receive Christ or send you more info. We would notify local pastors and Christian workers to call and follow up on you.

It was brilliant and I loved it. The testimonies were awesome and the reported numbers were staggering. But to this day I have never heard even one testimony of someone who was saved from it. Now I'm sure that there is still people serving God from this effort, probably many, I just haven't heard of them. You see I do not think that the banquet was ready or very good, it is also possible that the servants *"sent to compel"* did not *"compel"* or even go to the *"highways and hedges"*. Many just answered a phone.

Many of the invited guests had other reasons why they could not attend. For those that did, was there a feast of the abundant life that is promised with these affairs? Is the church and the servants doing the inviting, offering up food and fare that the invitees even want or need? Do the *"blind and lame, poor and crippled"* just get to remain *"blind and lame, poor and crippled?"* Do the highway wanderers just continue to wander spiritually or do they receive a message that is spiritually relevant to their lives? Is it to know God and know his love, or is it church growth? Is the banquet we set before the invitees relevant? Is the church of Jesus Christ relevant? Am I relevant? Does a person who prays on a phone really have their life changed or even understand what that means to give your life into the hands of Jesus. When their life doesn't change do they then say "been there and done that?"

I am the *"highways and hedges"* person, the *"crippled and the lame"*, I am the *"poor in spirit"* who has been *"Blessed"* and I have attended a very abundant feast in the Kingdom of God. It is relevant to me because I eat what is before me. I am very grateful to be here, I love the One who made it possible. I behave as an invited guest giving honor where honor is due to the Master of the Feast. He has adopted me in and made me his servant and sent me out to *"compel"* others, many who have excuses, some who don't believe that I have anything to set before them. They have already "been there and done that." So I go out to them with samples, sending my team to do outreaches, with free prayer. They go to the homeless camps to compel them to come to the feast. There is healing and wholeness in our Father's house. His presence dwells in our lives and in our worship, he resides in our gatherings and in our hearts. It is Jesus who has been the way maker, for us to know Him and hear Him and feel Him.

Won't you come and see the glory that is the Father of heaven and earth, and feast at His banqueting table?

First, SEE JESUS, then He will reveal to you the love of the Father.

That was His goal in the Pharisee's house and that is His goal today. First know who Jesus is, know His words and His deeds, give honor to Him and His purpose. Then see the Father and be loved. This is the feast and this is the purpose of the church. To be a banquet hall for the abundance of God's love and grace.

Is it your church that the invited guest can feast at? Do you go and "*compel*" them to come, are they the "*highways and hedges*" wanderer, the "*blind, crippled and the lame,*" "*the poor in spirit?*"

If they come will they stay the way they are or will they be "s*aved, healed and delivered?*"

CHAPTER 32

Christ Like

JESUS INTENDED that we become like Him, the very name Christian means that we would be little versions of Him. The Apostles understood this and there are many quotes of Jesus that make it clear. We should first follow or imitate Jesus and second imitate each other as we imitate Jesus.

Jesus is standing at the door knocking. He is making His home in us and Jesus is telling us that the things that we see Him do, we can do, even greater things than these can we do

He told us that if we believe, we could do anything, speak to anything or ask anything of our Father in heaven and it would be done for us. So, even if I cannot do it, our Father would do it for me. This sounds so good yet when I look around me this is not the reality that I see.

Something else Jesus asked was, when He returned would He find any faith left on the earth? I believe that I am living in the last days before Jesus returns, I must agree with Jesus that the evidence is not there to support that the Apostles were great men of faith at first nor is the evidence there to say that I am a great man of faith. The signs and wonders following me are just not as evident as they are in the stories of Jesus. The signs are indeed there, and I have told the stories of the people who are following me and are becoming like me as the evidence. They follow me as I become like Jesus, just not to the extent that Jesus promised they would be. I am *"striving to enter by the narrow door"* but I ask myself, am I living in the *"deep and wide"* life of the Kingdom of God? Some may ask what is that, this *"deep and wide"* life of the Kingdom? The answer, SEE JESUS, He is not only the *"narrow door"* that all must enter through, He is the *"deep and wide"* demonstration, He is the width and depth available to us who believe the words of Jesus. The promise that *"these things will you do and greater things than these will you do"* are the boundaries of the depth and width of the kingdom. More simply put, the width and breadth of the King of Kings is the boundary of what is available to you, the *"all things are possible to him who believes"* boundary.

I want more, so I ask myself these questions. Do we have the oil or Spirit filled churches talked about by the prophets when they saw the day that we would live in? A day when the presence of God is available to every one. When the curtain would be torn open and the glory of God would come out to us. Is this what Jesus was talking about when He said these things? That you could have what you asked for, get what you say, and when needed have the Father do for you, *"anything."* We could be filled with the very presence of the Holy God and Creator of Heaven and Earth. Do we have all that He intended for us to have?

I must ask myself daily what the enemies to my faith are and also what builds my faith? I do pray continually that the Lord would heal my wrong thinking and teach me more and more how I should live, and what in today's world is being Christlike. I pray that the Lord would heal my unbelief, sometimes it is desperate and I say "I believe, I believe, heal my unbelief." Then I look behind me to see if I have left a trail of signs and wonders, asking myself are the things that I said done? Are the things that I asked given? Then did my Father in Heaven do the things that I asked Him to? On more and more occasions He did do what I asked and signs and wonders are following me. This is absolute proof that my unbelief is being healed and my faith is more evident.

I have repented many times for making the failure all about my Father's unwillingness, instead of my lack of faith or my inability to imitate and be like Jesus. Saying things like "it must not be His will."

The bible says that He is perfect and I am being perfected. Then when something imperfect happens, even horrible, we blame the will of God as though the Father in heaven is there on His throne deciding if every prayer has merit or if the prayee is perfect enough. I think that some of these conclusions are so wrong that the church and her people will be very shocked to find out what was really in their power to affect on the earth. We will be shocked to find out how many actions on our part did not need a decision on His will but were expected. For instance, is it ever God's will that any of us who believe should not give love? Yet love is quite often not given by people who love God. Yet the only command in Christianity is to "love one another as I have loved you." So, just in that one example you can see how the will of God is affected by the will of man.

Jesus' promise is that we would do greater things than He did and "*whatsoever you ask*" would be done. He also said that whatever you say will be done, even to the point of commanding mountains and trees. If I can move a mountain because I believe and just because I say it, I then have to ask myself if that mountain was put there by God? Did His **will** put it there?

What did Jesus mean when He said "*ask whatsoever **you will** in my name.*" Can you and I really move a mountain placed there by **His will**? Did Jesus really put the dominion of **His will** in our hands? I think that is exactly what He means and if you accept this then you accept the responsibility that comes with it.

Your world will be "*saved, healed and delivered*" if you decide to do something about it. If there is any faith left on the earth when Jesus returns, it will have to be in you. Jesus says that *"all things are possible to you."* All that we see Jesus do and *"even greater things than these would you do."* This could become the standard of your expectation from your prayer life instead of accepting that only God's will gets done and it has nothing to do with our faith. Our Father has given His will into our hands to command even the mountains and trees, the wind and the waves, to rule the natural world with spiritual gifts which is the definition of *"Your Kingdom come, Your will be done, on earth as it is in Heaven."*

When I pray that God would heal the pain that I am experiencing, it would be ridiculous to think that the Father is on the throne deciding not to take the pain away. Like He would say "you just need to suffer a little longer", or "that just does not fit my plan". Instead, I believe that there is a pool of power provided and if I will tap into it with my faith then *"all things are possible,"* even the removal of my own pain. The power to remove pain is always available to me. This pool of power is the Holy Spirit. Healing power lives in me to do the Will of the Father. I know that the hope for a *"saved, healed and delivered"* world is our faith. The Lord trusts us and our will with His power, that we would accomplish His will which seldom changes. His will has not changed in two thousand years, He came to *"save, heal and deliver that which was lost."*

As we *"become children of God"* we begin to understand just how much of the church's success with the power and the message of the cross is put into the hands of the church. If we are to learn to live this kind of expectation in our prayer life, we are going to have to learn to celebrate and testify to what He is doing instead of what He is not doing. We must base our life's expectations on the truth of His promises. Are you in pain? Can I pray for you? If nothing happens then pray for the next one, and the next one after that until you start having testimonies that strengthen your faith.

When I pray for people I start by imitating Jesus and I say *"thank you Father that you hear me."* I have tried to stop saying "Father please heal," and started saying to the disease "The Lord has sent me" or "I come in the name of Jesus, go",to the disease, or I say to the person, "be healed". I have found when I tell a person this, then I lay hands on them they feel something which helps them believe, then I begin to thank God for what I want to happen. They do get healed more often when I apply my will and they feel the Holy Spirit's response to my words.

This seems to inspire faith and faith is what it takes to access this pool of power. Some people describe this pool as a room full of healthy parts that are ours for the taking. I am not sure what word picture you want, but I believe that the power of God is at the disposal of those who will live by faith. You will begin to create a culture of faith around you that will spread to your church and beyond, even to your world.

CHAPTER 33

Do Something

IN MATTHEW chapter 14 is the story of Jesus walking on the water. My favorite thing about Peter saying to Jesus, "*command me to come*" and then getting out of the boat and actually walking on water, is that he actually does it.

The number one difference between people who imitate Jesus and those that don't is that those who imitate Jesus, imitate Jesus, and those who don't imitate Jesus just don't.

I heard it said once that the difference between people who **do something** and people who **do nothing** is that people who do something, **do something.**

Peter walked on water and all I ever hear in sermons is that he looked at the waves and got scared. Peter walked on the water, **he did it** man, **he did it.** If even for a moment he imitated Jesus, it was so miraculous that we are still hearing about it today. Peter gets a lot of credit for what he failed at, but what I like to celebrate about him is what he did do. I would follow Peter any day and in fact I do. I call what he wrote the Word of God, and I follow it as God's command to me.

That is the kind of inspiration that I want to be to those who *"follow me as I follow Christ."*

I don't want them looking for signs and wonders as proof that God loves them or proof of his existence. I want them looking behind them after their lifestyle to see that signs and wonders are following them as a sign of their faith, and their imitation of Jesus. I want them to see that where they have gone, there are signs and wonders left behind because they were there. People were healed and fed and comforted, people were served.

If I will believe that God loves someone so much that He wants them healed,and they believe that He loves them so much He wants them healed, then their healing should be done according their faith in the fact that God loves them. Knowing who He is and who I am is the key to believing that what I ask is already done.

Knowing that the Father loves me and knowing that the Father loves them is probably the most important element to faith that I know! Believing the words of Jesus and hearing the Word of God as the Apostle told us is the truth. This is how my faith grows. When I ask for something and it does not happen, I must continue to pursue what I know to be true. If that truth is the Father's love, then my expectation will be at its highest and my faith will find it is riding on a greased skid. And then the proverbial ball is in my court and I must decide if I am going to do something.

Dee is my office manager. I remember when I first met her. I had returned from one of my visits to the "Toronto Blessing" where we frolicked in the power and presence of the Lord. The next Sunday I was leading worship. Dee's son had been born again, again. He was dancing in a most peculiar way and worshiping and manifesting the Holy Spirit all over the front row. His name is Mike and Mike had invited his mother. I remember seeing her behind him smiling. She got it, Mike was acting in a very strange manner. Most people frown and look very uncomfortable when they first see it. Dee was smiling so big and so happy to see her son was back loving Jesus. I am sure she did think it was strange, but she got it, that the most important thing was his incredible joy and love for the Lord.

Dee knew that her son was lost, but now he is alive. If this is God, then it really does not matter what it looks like, it's God. The joy and worship are good signs of this. As time went on Mike proved to be the fruit that remains and is a world changer. Mike is a son to the Father. A lover of God, a friend to Jesus.

Right after this day I had an opening in my construction company, Dee applied for the job. We hired her, and that may have been the last day that the job was ever just the office manager of a construction company.

When I would go to restaurants in Oroville or to school athletic events people would ask me "doesn't gramma Dee work for you?" Or they would say that they know me because gramma Dee works for me. I began to find out that I did not hire just any qualified office worker. God had sent me a gift. A very special gift. He could have sent gramma Dee to anyone, He sent her to me. When she is at a school game or shopping at the local stores, Dee is approached by many who come over to act like they are there to give love. I watch, I know that they are there because they know that if they approach Dee they will receive love. She never disappoints them.

The name of the business should have been Steve Orsillo Enterprises because it was right after Dee came that we started The Father's House Church. This led to the rental company, the real estate company, a second non-profit called Intercept Oroville.

Dee took over Vicki and my personal bills. My kids who were involved in sports and every other activity in Oroville would call Dee for help, so she became Orsillo central control, picking them up and dealing with their problems. Answering phone calls from Mark which can be lots of calls. All this, while handling the mountain of invoices, insurance papers, contracts, bank accounts. Plus, she took over all of the real estate loans. Also biggest time bandit of them all, employees.

We had twenty of them plus thirty subcontractors all handled legally to ensure a mountain of paperwork.

Now try to believe this, the church grows to a campus of twelve buildings and thirty staff, hundreds of people. It is amazing what happened. As it all grew to become this, Dee just absorbed it all. I never had to worry about any of it. She needed me to make the decisions and she took care of the rest. When I was out of town I would call in, we would go over all of the questions, Dee would handle it all.

People ask me all the time; How do you do what you do? The team around me is the answer. The captain of that team is Dee.

The world famous crash of the real estate market hit Oroville about three years ago in the year 2006. The stress became knee buckling, it was also very hard to understand what was going on with the provision of God. I could see the stress on Dee. I don't believe it was about money, I believe that it was her worrying about me.

Dee kept asking me about the future. What was I going to do about her employment? Did I want her to work less hours? What I would tell her was that I thought the Lord was not going to let us go down. She would then lift me up and tell me what a faithful man I had been. God would come through for us, but what do you want to do 'now'? I would tell her that she was not replaceable, not only that, there was no human I had ever met who could do what she does.

We would sell a truck or tractor, pay this bill or those bills. Rebates on the canceled insurances or the rents would come in and I would pay Dee. The inevitable day did come. I had to lay Dee off. She had worked for me for eleven years. There was no darker day for me than that day. I am sure it was no picnic for her either.

What would I do? I thought of taking the mountains of files out with some gasoline, make a good fire then seek asylum in a foreign country. Forget about it!

In the morning the sun did rise. Dee showed up. She said all this work had to be done, she knew that I would be lost. She has done the church's books and paper work from day one. She said "who else would do it"? She has showed up and donated her time ever since.

The Father's House Church is the work of so many people. People often give Vicki and I the credit for what has happened to south Oroville. There are many who deserve the credit. None more than Dee. There are so many people that this church has blessed. Almost none of them would know Dee. She does not do this for the credit.

She does not attend The Father's House. Dee goes to church at the same church she went to when I first met her. The Oroville Church of the Nazarene is Dee's church. She loves Jesus and she gives without the thought of herself.

When I define the Christlike nature as "selflessness", and then I start to describe people who "WOULD DO SOMETHING", and when I talk about the command of Christ as "loving one another", heck, if you want to see the very definition of the "Christlike", "do Something", "she would" nature, or the model for "Living and Loving Jesus" *a life lived being Christian*, I suggest that you "SEE DEE."

Vicki and I know that we would not be very far along on the vision that God has given us, if not for Dee. Thanks Dee! Thanks Jesus for sending her to us.

The difference between someone who does something and someone who does nothing is this. The person who does something, "DOES SOMETHING."

CHAPTER 34

Do you give a "Blank"

JESUS SAID that to see someone hungry and to not feed them was a failure on the level of being kicked out of the kingdom, because it was the same thing as not feeding Jesus.

Many years ago a man named Anthony (Tony) Campolo came on the scene and was the hot preacher in the Christian circles that I was hanging out in. We were reading his books and going to large venues to hear him speak.

Anthony Campolo touched us, he preached the message of Jesus and to this day I am still inspired by what he did during his so called fifteen minutes of fame.

An example that will help you understand the power of his message and the condition of the Christian church happened in Sacramento, California. I was a youth pastor at the time and went to Arco Arena to hear him, the place was full. I know it held seventeen thousand people for basketball games but they would fill the floor as well for speakers so there was more people than that on this night.

He was telling about the horrible condition of living that children around the world were having to endure. At one point he said, "while I am speaking, twenty thousand children will die of starvation around the world." Tony paused for effect and then he said, "I said, while I am speaking, twenty thousand children will die of starvation and you people just don't give a BLANK," now he didn't say blank, he cussed. He said just what you think he said. He said it to more than seventeen thousand church going Christian people.

The air was sucked out of the room. Tony paused for a even bigger effect. People did not know what to do. His words were echoing through my head and I was too stunned to speak or move. He only paused for seconds and it seemed like minutes had passed when he began again. "I said that twenty thousand children will die of starvation and all you care about is that I said BLANK." A collective moan began to grow in the crowd as the conviction of the Holy Spirit began his good work in us. The religious spirits went into hyperdrive. I waited for the cries of "crucify him" to begin, these cries did not come on this night, they did not rise from me. The Holy Spirit was changing me right there on the concrete floor of Arco Arena. The priorities of what is important and what is not began to be life to me.

The words of Jesus that *"blessed are the hungry for they will be fed"* I now understood to mean more than food. I was hungry and my spirit was fed this night. I was fed with the fact that while living in His church I had gone to sleep and forgot to keep His priorities and had failed to remember that hungry children are the concern of the church.

That was the fact that Anthony Campolo had hit me with, right between the eyes. I really did hear the cuss word and it was really all that I cared about. He did not say that his car broke down and we did not give a "blank". He said children were starving to death. It had passed me by. But not now, the Holy Spirit has brought me to my knees. I repent, I am turned around.

The Pharisees had no answer on this night, just like in Luke 14 when Jesus asked *"is it good to heal this man on the sabbath?"*

My life was changed and even though Tony Campolo has never met me, everything that I have done in my life since has brought honor and credit to his courage and obedience. The conviction of the Holy Spirit has had its wonderful effect in me.

On the day when the kingdom is gathered together and the sheep and the goats are separated, I will be a sheep. I believe that I have seen him hungry and with all that I have, I have tried to feed him.

It is people who have invested in me like Tony Campolo though he does not know it, and John Arnott, Sister Aimee, the Partners in Harvest pastors and leaders and Pastor Joe Wittwer from Life Center Church in Spokane Washington, who have done something in me. I am grateful to them for the investment that has produced the spiritual return that is known as The Father's House Church.

The real return is the staff and volunteers of The Father's House Church who see the *"hungry"* and the *"thirsty"*, the *"naked"* and *"imprisoned"* and they **"do something."** They **"give a blank"**!!!

CHAPTER 35

I Work for Jesus

I AM sitting here on a day that is as beautiful as any that I have seen, basking in the love that I have found in the Father's arms. As is my habit I am saying to Him, "here I am Father, I am with you, I know that you see me and I know that you can hear me, yet I don't want anything, just to be with you and know you better." As I do my usual morning greeting, a flood of memories comes to me and it is as if my life is flashing before my eyes.

The memory of my first ministry is playing over in my mind as I see that it ended poorly with me being asked not to come back to any youth events outside of my local church because the denomination thought that I was dangerous.

You see, I believed in speaking in tongues and that was a very disruptive belief to them. I also raised both hands in worship and when the songs stopped playing I would continue in my worship, so then I was a marked man. I had never told any youth that I believed in speaking in tongues because I knew of their different belief. The pastor and I discussed it and he wanted me to stay but I could not go to multi-church functions. I would have to send my group with someone else. That was not realistic, so I had to go.

I later found out that the pastor had been fooling around with women in his church. It was my first time that a pastor had failed in his own personal life in front of me. As I look back I realize that I learned from this time and ministry. I was thankful to the Lord for it, not for the fact that the pastor failed, but for the ministry that I had, the friendships that I enjoyed and the growth in spiritual things. I was also thankful for a very clear realization or revelation that, "I work for Jesus." That doesn't make me callous to the pain that is caused by this man's failure. Those results just don't have to take me down a notch or cause me to have a faith crisis.

At this same time I was working in a framing company of carpenters for a man who was as crude as any person that I have ever known. He never referred to a woman in any way that was not horrible. He called anyone who didn't talk in the nastiest way about women a terrible name. In all the time that I worked for him the only way that I could be sure that he knew my name was that he wrote it on my paychecks. He called me the **blank** (and he did not say blank.) It is a part of the anatomy. He would say to the lead man, "you and the **blank** go and do this or that." It did not matter what it was he was saying, he would refer to me in this derogatory word. He never spoke a kind word in all that time. The atmosphere on that job was very hard. Big guys picking on little guys and everybody racing each other trying to get the bosses favor, yet that was not going to happen. At best, you just might not be the focus of his crudeness.

Now I bet you wonder what would make anybody stay in that situation. It was the fact that in spite of the horrible working conditions, this man had the best framing system that I had ever seen or could believe was possible. I would learn this system and use it. I eventually did leave and found myself looking for work. I approached a contractor to ask for a job. He asked me how much money I wanted to make per hour. I said "eight dollars an hour." He said there was no way he could pay that much money. Then I offered to work for half a day for free, I said, "if you do not think that I am worth eight dollars then we can just go our separate ways and you will owe me nothing". He agreed. A half hour after I started working he came and said, "you got your eight dollars." About a week later he asked if I would be his foreman and teach all of his men my system.

I have used this system all of my life and made a great deal of money for whoever I worked for, also for me and my family. All I had to do was put up with this man who belittled me and treated me like less than human. I tried to tell him how real the Lord was, but then he would even get worse towards me and ridicule me to people in restaurants. I was able to get what he had and that was great. I think that God sent me there to get it. My Father wanted me to have it. All I had to do was *work as unto the Lord.* I did have to remind myself often saying to myself "I work for Jesus", "I work for Jesus". I even clicked my heels together while I said it hoping to wake up from this nightmare. When other people would ask me why I put up with him I would say, "I work for Jesus and this is where he has me."

Here I am thirty four years later. I think often of the blessings in my life, what I have seen and been part of. I have really earned a lot of money for me and for the ministries that my wife and I have supported. We have had a great deal and we have had darn near nothing in our lives. Vicki and I have seen the loaves and fishes miracle in our finances and in our ministry. The training I received at this job has been a constant source of income throughout our lives. We continually remember that we have been *saved, healed and delivered* into the hand of a most loving God and we really do "work for Jesus." We have had leaders in business and leaders in church that have been very bad. Some have been evil even. Others are hurt so deeply that they cannot do anything but hurt other people. We try to remember, "we work for Jesus."

We once spent four years at a church we were sent to by the district supervisor of the denomination to help the pastor. This pastor was so threatened by the supervisor's praise of us that he spent four years telling us how much he loved us and pretending to be our friend, all the while working behind the scenes to discredit us. I can tell you that this was very hard when we found out. Many people actually hated us and would use those words to us saying, "I hate you so." In fact, in a "if you have ought against your brother" message we would just begin to say that the line forms to the right, and it would.

That pastor finally got caught with other women and stealing from the church, and left town. We worked for Jesus and had done nothing but be faithful to our commitments, and that pastor. We really gained from the experience, we have hope and compassion for that pastor's family.

Vicki and I have also had great leaders, we have grown so much from them, we have always been impressed by their love for Jesus. Whether with great leaders or some that really need healing, we have always "worked as unto the lord," laboring day and night for the love of the saints and the promotion and growth of his kingdom. Always and in everything giving thanks to the Lord.

CHAPTER 36

Sons and Daughters

SOMEWHERE IN our lives we really became the keepers of the vineyard that is often referred to by Jesus. The standers in the gap. The ones the Lord looks to and fro across the face of the earth looking for.

He showed us the difference between being bond servants or hirelings as opposed to being sons and daughters. When trouble comes, the hireling runs. I have done that a few times in my life, though not anymore.

The sons of the master of the vineyard know the vineyard is their father's and they say things like, "not on my watch" or "over my dead body." They see trouble through, understanding that this vineyard is their vineyard, even their life. Like the Apostle said *"where would we go Lord,"* we say "you hold the keys to TRUTH and LIFE," I am not going anywhere. This church is worth fighting for. This truth is worth fighting for. This kingdom is the kingdom of my Father and He has put me in the inheritance with my older brother Jesus.

The prodigal had a similar revelation, when he said that the servants eat better in his father's house than he did in life's pig-pens. He would rather be a pig-pen keeper in his father's house than to continue to do it for these strangers. He went home, only to have his father receive him back as a son.

I understand this very well because I had been a bond servant of Jesus Christ for many years. I have been taken in as a son of my Father and I submit to working along side the bond servants because I want them to see the privilege of sonship. I was so happy being just a bond servant and it was a good life. It is a really good life and the servants really do live better than the pigs. I would know since I spent some time in the pig-pens of life. Now that I have seen the vision of being allowed to "become the children of God," I don't want to be just a bond servant who will run from hard work or hard situations, instead I want to be a son. My lifestyle of believing in Him and believing in His death and resurrection has caused God to make me His son. WOW!!!

King David said, "*I would rather be a doorkeeper in the house of the Lord than to dwell in the tents of the wicked.*" He saw that being chosen by God was a very special calling and was to be respected and honored. Even being a servant in the Father's tabernacle is a good thing. David knew that being anointed by God was better. God would call him, "*my servant David.*" We all know of David's very publicized imperfections, yet God called him His servant. David would probably dream about meeting God's Son, never about being God's son. The Apostle understood that to those who believe He gave them the power to become children of God. A title that was probably unimaginable to people of David's day.

Peter denied Jesus three times and upon His resurrection Jesus said to the ladies who found Him, "go to My brethren and say to them, I ascend to My Father and your Father, and My God and your God." He tells them and includes Peter by name that "*my Father will be their Father.*" You just don't leave a son out because he is not perfect, now that is a position that I can get into. I do certainly qualify, imperfect and eager and I believe, I have them all, and I am a lover of God and Jesus the one He sent.

Now, if I can just get into this "*loving one another as He has loved me*," "*forgiving as I have been forgiven*." Then being a "*joint heir with Jesus*" is the promise that I can sink my teeth into.

CHAPTER 37

A Shepherd, A Housewife and A Coin

THE PRODIGAL son is a very interesting story that is one of the stories that we do hear preached often. Yet we only hear a portion of the message that Jesus was preaching. He starts with a lost sheep, then tells about a lost coin, followed up by the wayward son, all the while really not focusing or trying to tell us about a sheep, coin or a son. This is a story about a Father.

I know that Jesus says it is a good shepherd, a housewife and a son. The real story here, is that this Father watches the horizon, runs to his son, gives him honor and authority, (the ring and robe).

The shepherd leaves his flock and searches for his lost sheep. He rejoices when he finds it, he loves it and restores it to its place. This is not a lesson on how to shepherd sheep, it is a lesson on how much the Father loves you.

The lost coin is very valuable and was lost in carelessness. The housewife sweeps everything and looks everywhere, until she finds the coin, then she brags to her friends and celebrates. Again this is not a story titled "with Christ in the school of housewifeing", it is a story of "With Christ in the school of the Father's Love".

The sheep wandered off not necessarily on purpose and that is something many of us can relate to. We end up asking the question "how did I get here"? We say "I think that I am lost".

The coin was lost without its help. It was the lack of care by others. I look at the people in my church and then all over the world for that matter. I ask "how did they get so lost, what did they do to deserve this"? With the vast majority of these people they had nothing to do with it. They were bred and raised to end up where they were. They were born in unfair circumstances. The current of their life took them and they didn't know any better. Misery seems to them to be God's will for them.

The prodigal made a bad choice. He was wooed by the money and the life money could bring him. He was tempted, he sinned and found himself in a very tough circumstance. More than a few of the people that I know can relate to this situation. I zigged when I shoulda zagged, and we find that the grass really was not greener on the other side.

No matter how we get lost or separated from His love, whether it is through being born in unfair circumstances, rebellion or carelessness, our fault or not, if it is the choices of other people or our own selfishness, the real story here that Jesus is preaching is the Father is looking for your return to Him. Not so He can say "its about time" but to call His friends together and throw parties. To those of us who get lost from time to time, for whatever reason, it is good to know that our Father is looking for us. He is not just tolerating us but He genuinely loves us and is looking for our return, watching, searching, even sweeping away the things that would hide us from Him. Going out to find us, pursuing us, and yes even carrying us home.

So whether you were lost because you rebelled or you were born in unfair circumstances or maybe you just wandered off, it's even possible you don't know how you got lost. The real story here for you is that the Father of heaven and Lord over all of the earth, your Father, loves you and He is pursuing you. He is not casually glancing to see if you're coming but watching, searching and waiting to give you another chance. Your Father sent Jesus to die for you so that He could get you back from the world that does not take care of your heart.

Your Father has sent me, not a servant, me His son, to tell you that He loves you. He has many sons and daughters that He has sent to you. Our Father really does want you to come home to Him.

These stories about a sheep, a coin and a lost son are really stories of the Father's love for His lost children. He rejoices at their return. No matter how you relate to Jesus' stories about being lost, relate to this. The Father is the good shepherd, the diligent housewife, and the watching Father who restores honor, authority and brings love back into our lives.

Call on Him, seek Him, ask Him to take away your sins and be forgiven. Place your life in the hands of the loving Father. He will receive you, He is looking for you on the horizon, come home.

CHAPTER 38

The Kingdom as a Son

I THINK of the Kingdom of Heaven as an inheritance, and I think of the Kingdom of Heaven as a place to reside in, complete with God's will being done here on earth just as it is in heaven. I think about the Kingdom of Heaven from the prospective of being the King's son. Does that make me a prince? I wonder if people see me as a prince of the Lord of Heaven and King over all of the earth? I have to answer the question for myself as well, do I see myself as a prince?

People come to my church and they leave just as sick as they came. This is not okay with me and it is not what is supposed to happen in the Kingdom of the Father God. People come addicted and they are supposed to do the one step program to recovery. They are supposed to get healed at the altar when they are forgiven, the gospel is supposed to set them free. They are supposed to be *"born again"* made brand new. I ask myself if this is even my expectation when I minister? I do expect it more often when I feel like a prince than I did when I felt like a bond servant.

The ministry to the addicted is not supposed to be as hard as it is but the Lord said *"be it done unto you according to your faith."* The church is only going to be as powerful as the people's beliefs. My job as a son is to try to make an atmosphere of the Kingdom that reveals the Father's love and teaches the word of God in a way that promotes faith in the hearing and believing of the message of Jesus. The most important part of this job is to teach the truth about God. It is not to try to get people to have more faith since it only requires a mustard seed sized faith to move an actual mountain. It is getting them to believe that He has put the power in their hands. It is getting them to know that *"all things are possible to him who believes."* If we walk as sons of our Father we know that all authority has been put in our hands to bring the Kingdom, preach the Kingdom and to walk in the Kingdom. We will lift up Jesus because He is our source for this inheritance. He will draw all men to the message of His Salvation.

It is only done when the church stops promoting unbelief through the failures of the leaders and the teaching that everything is dependent on the will of God, saying it will only happen if it's God's will. As if it's not His will to set people free. As if Jesus endured the cross so that the Kingdom would not reign.

Jesus asked, "IS IT GOOD TO HEAL THIS MAN"? Do we answer any better than the Pharisee's did? Jesus asked if any of us who were living in our sin nature would have withheld any good thing from our sons? Then how can we believe that the Heavenly Father would fail to give any good thing to His sons? To believe this we think God is less good than we are. To be a son is to understand our Father's heart. It is His will to give us the good things that are apparent in His Kingdom, like food, clothing and miraculous things like healing and power, and in abundance too. It is not the Christmas list of wishes that we had as children hoping we would receive what we asked for. It is already purchased for us and we must use our faith to believe that we are His children and our Father bought them for us.

Jesus went to the cross to forgive, and set the captives free. It is always His will to forgive. It seems this is where our faith always ends. Jesus went to the cross to pay for our sins, but He also went to the whipping post to cause our healing. The prophet said *"by His stripes we are healed,"* why is this so hard to believe and forgiveness so easy.? Forgiveness causes you to believe, healing causes belief to spread, failure in healing causes faith to become feeble and weak, weak faith causes failure in healing. We do have an enemy to our faith, and faith is what causes the Kingdom to come, His will to be done, here as it is there in heaven.

We at The Father's House will continue to work within people's faith, we will also expect that the Lord will set them free in the confession of their faith. But most of all we will continue to dig and burn and burn and dig to understand and then believe that we are sons and daughters of the Lord of Heaven and King over all the earth and that this Lord and King is our Father, our Daddy, and He will not withhold any *"good thing"* from us.

It is not alright to have people believe that in praying for the sick, the addicted or the hopeless, they will not recover based on, "it must not be God's will." It is His Kingdom and in the Kingdom of Heaven it is always His will and everyone who believes gets healed. We must decide if this is true if we are going to minister in the Kingdom of God.

It is time to decide who we have been *"born again"* to become. Believing in our identity causes faith to move mountains. It does not take much faith to get healed. If the amount doled out to each man is enough, then the problem must be in who is using this faith. In the gospel Jesus knows who He is and what His Father's will is and many get healed by Him. It is those who won't believe in His identity that don't get healed. A mustard seed of faith can move a mountain, can my faith believe that it is always God's will to set people free from sin, sickness and bondage like addiction?

I have become increasingly aware that one more thing is very important for people to get healed when I pray for them. They must believe that I am God's son as well. The Lord showed us that a prophet is not without honor except among his own people and that is why traveling preachers and strangers with big reputations cause more miracles than a pastor at his own church. It is hard to believe that people whose imperfections we have seen are anointed to bring healing. It's hard to believe they could be sons of the Living God. Listen to the testimonies when people are healed or have experienced miracles they will say this man has something, or he is so anointed. They receive powerful results because the preacher believes he has come with something powerful and the receiver believes the preacher has come with something powerful. If the Kingdom is to reign here on earth just as it does in God's presence, then first we must believe that it is His will. We must also believe that we are more than bond servants, sons even, joint heirs with Jesus. In addition people seeking God's power must believe that we have the authority and anointing. People's perspective of who we are is very important, in fact I believe these are the missing ingredients in the day to day demonstration of His power in our world.

Why did the disciples leave their nets and follow Jesus? Because He was anointed by God, He had a recognizable anointing. Jesus did many miracles that did not require other people's belief, these miracles helped other people recognize who Jesus was. He turned water into wine and raised dead people, calmed storms, demons spoke to Him as He entered their presence. These were all events that only required His knowledge of His identity, but revealed to others that He had something, He had an anointing, He was someone to believe in and He is still today. If we recognize this and come to a understanding of who He is, can we then believe in who that makes us? The question is, can we believe ?

Can my faith believe: THAT IT REALLY IS GOOD TO HEAL THIS MAN, AND GOD DOES WANT TO?

Can my faith believe that God has made me His Son, and this is what it takes to have the *"Kingdom come His will be done on earth as it is in Heaven?"*

If my faith can believe that God has allowed me to become His son then this belief challenges me to behave as a son behaves. I will be taking on the responsibility of sonship as my standard of behavior. I must seek to learn how a son behaves in the world. Then people who are watching will have less trouble believing that Jesus has come to do good things for them and make them new creatures. If I accept this standard of behavior people will have less trouble believing that I am God's son, they will have less obstacles to believing that they also can become children of God. Good things like freedom, joy, goodness and mercy, God's favor and many, many more things will begin to be the expectation of those who believe. IT REALLY IS GOOD TO DO THESE THINGS AND GOD DOES WANT THEM DONE.

CHAPTER 39

Just Keep Living and Loving Jesus

THE LIFE that we have experienced seems to me to be unbelievable! I doubt in fact that everyone who reads it does believe it. I have not been able to write half of what our experiences have been. If I did, it would take me a lifetime to write it down.

Since I started trying to write down an account of what God has done in our lives simply because we have believed in His name and lived our lives as an expression of love for Jesus, so many blessings have been added to us and so many fruitful days have come and gone. So many, many people have come through our lives and left their mark on us and deposited love to our account.

I am so excited that I can hardly wait to see what God has in store for us, I guess that I will have to wait though. In the meantime I will just go on **"LIVING AND LOVING JESUS."**

Kingdom Awakening Apprenticeship

KINGDOM AWAKENING APPRENTICESHIP is aimed towards individuals who desire to know more about the Living God and expand their expectation of who He is and who they are as sons and daughters of God.

The environment of the apprenticeship is community and discipleship to help students understand their role in the Kingdom of God and how it relates to the world in which they live.

In addition to class time, students serve in a ministry in the church. There, they serve experienced leaders where they are mentored and inspired to reach the church body and surrounding community. We are compelled by the words of Jesus to His disciples: "as my Father has sent me, I am sending you".

We are committed to develop willing people who have the passion to see a generation move towards true love, true hope and true faith.

Kingdom Awakening Apprenticeship begins with a 6-month Core School where students learn the simplicity and importance of the gospel. Students are then promoted to an additional 6-month internship to practically apply what they have learned. There is also opportunity to move on to 2nd and 3rd year internship.

To learn more please visit **www.kingdomawakening.com**, e-mail **kingdomawakening@live.com** or call **1-800-394-1150**.

MORE FATHER'S HOUSE CHURCH MINISTRIES

Life Recovery Ministries

LIFE RECOVERY MINISTRIES is a 12-month Christian Discipleship home where men and women who suffer from the disease of addiction can be in a safe place, designed to help turn lives and wills over to the care and control of our Lord Jesus Christ.

Our goal is to have alcohol and drug free men and women who have a strong relationship with Jesus Christ, functioning in a positive manner towards their families and society.

If you are interested please call Danny Harp at (530) 534-4704 or (530) 370-5587

Or you can write us at **The Father's House Church, 2661 Elgin St, Oroville, Ca 95966**

CONTACT INFORMATION

Pastor Steve Orsillo
The Father's House Church
530-534-4140
Tfhc-oroville.org
2661 Elgin St. Oroville California 95966

To PURCHASE more copies of this book or to just correspond with pastor Steve, email pastorsteveorsillo@gmail.com or call the number above and place an order.

WATCH FOR Steve Orsillo's new book "*Follow Me*". A book about the call of Jesus to follow Him and what that means and what it looks like, as we live in obedience to His call.

www.ingramcontent.com/pod-product-compliance
Lightning Source LLC
Chambersburg PA
CBHW020857090426
42736CB00008B/412